CW00983714

Times subject to Tides

The Story of Barra Airport

Roy Calderwood

Times subject to Tides

The Story of Barra Airport

by

Roy Calderwood

© Roy Calderwood 1999

British Library Cataloguing in Publication Data
Calderwood, Roy
Times subject to Tides: The Story of Barra Airport
1. Barra Airport – History 2. Aeronautics, Commercial – Scotland – Barra - History
I. Title
387.7'36'094114
ISBN 0 9518958 3 4

Published by
Kea Publishing
14 Flures Crescent, Erskine, Renfrewshire PA8 7DJ, Scotland

Printed by
Iain M. Crosbie Printers
Beechfield Road, Willowyard Industrial Estate, Beith, Ayrshire KA15 1LN

All rights reserved. No part of this publication may be reproduced, stored in a retrieval system or transmitted in any form or by any means without prior permission from the author and publisher.

For all who love Barra

but especially Harold and Brenda

Times subject to Tides

Contents

Maps

Foreword

by

Dr Winifred M Ewing MA LLB FRSA
Member of the European Parliament for the Highlands and Islands of Scotland, 1979-1999
Member of the Scottish Parliament for the Highlands and Islands, 1999 -

Barra is a magic island in a magic sea of islands.

Landing by air on its cockle strand is one of the best air experiences in Europe. The sense of clean air and space is like heady wine.

On landing you can see the home of the late Compton Mackenzie, Scots writer and patriot. His book Whisky Galore, based on a true story, is legendary. The landing is just an introduction to an island of beautiful bays and crofts and townships with Castlebay, the proud capital. Kishmuls Castle is one of the reminders of our European connection with the Vikings and one can almost see the laden galleys arriving.

If time permits, visitors can pay respects to Compton who lies buried at Eoligarry.

The people of Barra are famous for singing and gumption and many songs relate to this piece of earth including The Fair Maid of Barra whom I often visited.

From Barra one can visit another beautiful island, Vatersay, by causeway - who knows, perhaps if Objective One European Funding continued, we should soon also be able to walk over to Eriskay, where Charlie landed.

Barra is a place not only to visit but to live in and a part of my heart will always be there.

Winifred M Ewing

Pictured opposite Loganair's de Havilland Twin Otter, G-BVVK, in May 1997. (Photo by John Rice from his book The Dream of Night Fishers (Scottish Cultural Press, Edinburgh, 1998))

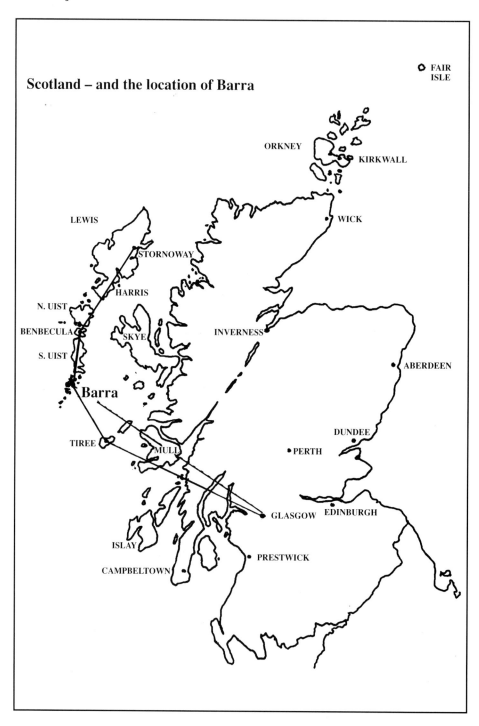

Scotland – and the location of Barra

Introduction

"It is no unusual occurrence to find as many as twenty or thirty horses..and ponies..moving hither and thither across this great sandy stretch (Tràigh Mhòr) at one time. And in the heat of the noon day sun they appear afar off like a tribe of nomads trekking with their impedimenta across an Eastern desert." *Summer Days among the Western Isles*, A A MacGregor, 1929.

It was not long after this quotation was written that aircraft started to visit Barra's great beach. While the equine traffic has disappeared, the aeronautical variety still descends over Northbay on a regular basis.

It was in June 1936, at the same time as a small grass airfield in Sussex opened its first passenger terminal on land next to Gatwick racecourse, that a fledgling Scottish airline first introduced calls on demand at Barra in Scotland's Western Isles. Whereas the Sussex airfield developed into a great international airport, the Tràigh Mhòr at Barra has seen less change but continues to provide a valuable community facility. Through the vision of such early airline pioneers as Fresson, Sword and Nicholson, islands were among the first places in the UK to benefit from air transport and few would deny that Barra would be the poorer without its air link.

Loganair's DHC-6 Twin Otter, which now operates in the livery of British Airways, is just the latest in a long line of sturdy aircraft to have provided the essential link with Glasgow and the world. The schedule is still governed by the ebb and flow of the tide. The Tràigh Mhòr is surely one of the most beautiful locations in the Western Isles and, at low tide, this natural asset makes a superb "low impact" airport for Barra. All of the Tràigh Mhòr, which means 'Great Beach' and is pronounced "try-vore", and the isthmus between Ben Eoligarry to the north and Ben Vaslain to the south, are designated by Scottish Natural Heritage as a Site of Special Scientific Interest, such is the importance of the flora, fauna, and the beach's dune and machair system. The dazzling Tràigh Mhòr, with its "runways" made of nothing more than mineral detritus, is fringed on the landward side by sand dunes and hills, and seawards by a necklace of small islands including Orosay, Gighay and Hellisay.

Barra's air service, which might once have been considered a luxury, is now a highly valued asset of which the islanders are highly protective. Recent debate on the question of a hard runway makes this an opportune time to record the story of this unusual airfield. Times subject to Tides looks at the aviation history of the beach, beginning with Northern & Scottish Airways in 1936 and tracing developments through the twentieth century. Early chapters look at the location of the airfield and trace its use through a succession of operators and aircraft types. Further chapters provide a snapshot of some of the personalities who have been closely linked with the airfield, and look at the air ambulance service, the 1994 services by the Shorts 360 airliner, and current day to day operations. Fred Barnes gives a unique view of Heron operations to Barra from 1955 to 1973, and the story is concluded with a selection of appendices.

While other airport authorities are required to spend great sums of money making their airports environmentally friendly, the natural beauty of Tràigh Mhòr is unsullied by its use as Barra Airport, and long may this co-existence continue. If you have not already visited Barra, I hope you may soon be splashing down for the start of your own Hebridean adventure.

Roy Calderwood

Pastoral tranquillity at Barra's airport, c. 1948 (Photo: A. A. MacGregor, courtesy of the Scottish Life Archive, National Museums of Scotland)

De Havilland Dragons of Northern & Scottish Airways inaugurated scheduled services to Barra in 1936. The airline became Scottish Airways in 1937 and this Dragon, G-ACNG, was photographed on 24 May 1939. (John Stroud)

1

Barra, the Tràigh Mhòr, and the Importance of the Air Service

"The Twin Otter dipped its wing, put its nose hard down, and fell from 500 feet straight towards the beach. I knew it was going to happen, but it still sent my heart into my mouth..." Christopher Somerville writing in *The Other British Isles*, 1990.

Flying into Barra may be the stuff of travel writing but, primarily, the airport is there to improve the quality of life for those who live on the island. Sixty years after the air service was introduced, it is not difficult to appreciate the difference it must have made at the time of its inception. MacBraynes - who had been serving Barra since 1889 - had fairly recently introduced a new vessel called the Lochearn. This occurred in 1930 and followed the financial reconstruction of the company in 1928. The Outer Isles mail run was still a lengthy crossing. In June 1936, the vessel was casting off from Castlebay Pier three times a week on Tuesdays, Thursdays and Saturdays at the ungodly hour of 3.15am. With calls at Tiree, Coll, Kilchoan (Ardnamurchan) and Tobermory (Mull), the mail steamer finally landed its passengers at Oban nearly twelve hours later at 2.45pm. For the islander travelling to Glasgow, a further 117 miles lay ahead on the train journey via Callander and Stirling. With time to kill in Oban, the London Midland & Scottish Railway would be unlikely to set him down at Glasgow's Buchanan Street station much before 9.30pm following about four and a quarter hours on the train. Suddenly, islanders who could afford the air fare of £4 single, were able to avoid the often stormy sea crossing and the train journey. Now, within two hours, they could find themselves on the grass at Renfrew, "Airport for Glasgow", and just a short ride from the city centre.

The other major benefit throughout that time has been access to the air ambulance, a facility which started in 1933 with the evacuation from Islay of fisherman, John McDermid. As a doctor could now request the despatch of an aircraft from Renfrew to remove the patient to a city hospital, the fear of serious illness was immediately lessened with the arrival of the aeroplane. Over the years, many islanders have had good cause to be grateful to the pilots and nurses who have responded to emergency call-outs in all weathers, day and night.

Maps of Scotland reveal Barra's location near the southern end of the 200km chain of islands which form the Outer Hebrides, or Western Isles. Roughly 80km west of the Scottish mainland and stretching from the Butt of Lewis to Barra Head, which is on the Isle of Berneray, only twelve of the islands are still inhabited. They remain the last stronghold of the Gaelic language in Scotland.

Barra is about 13km long by 6.5km wide and has a population of around 1,300 gathered mostly in its small coastal townships. The largest of these is Castlebay, service centre for all of Barra and Vatersay, and which is located around one of the best natural harbours in the Hebrides. Here the Caledonian MacBrayne ferry makes its landfall in the shadow of Kisimul Castle several times each week to disgorge passengers, vehicles, and essential supplies at the end of the five-hour crossing from Oban. A circular road links the island townships with a spur serving Eoligarry. A new road and causeway, opened in 1991, links Barra and Vatersay.

Barra's hilly interior, part of a geological fault line called the Outer Hebrides Thrust, peaks on Heaval at 383 metres. The rocky, indented, eastern coastline is complemented by the machair of the west side and the Eoligarry peninsula in the north. During the long summer days, the machair, that grass sward behind the beaches which is unique to the Hebrides and some parts of western Ireland, hosts a prolific bird life and outstanding displays of wild flowers. Created when the shell sand is blown on to the Hebridean gneiss behind the dunes to mix with the soil, it is a rich and beautiful part of the natural heritage of the islands.

At the north end of Barra, the east and west coasts of the island come within yards of each other at the neck of the Eoligarry peninsula. The Tràigh Eais on the Atlantic, or west side, is backed by marram-covered dunes which are much eroded by wind, rain, cattle and rabbits, resulting in the redistribution of the sand over the isthmus. Across the machair and the Eoligarry road, over which the wind often carries the sand, is the Tràigh Mhòr.

Whether you see it for the first time, as I did, from the air, or perhaps from the road approach near Ardmhòr, you soon realise that this is one of the island's most stunning features. At low tide, the wide sands seem to stretch as far as the eye can see with smaller offshore islands fringing the strand like beached whales. By contrast, at high water it assumes the appearance of an inland sea, the water lapping only yards from the little airport terminal which is at the westernmost extremity of the beach.

Sixty years after the first aircraft landed here, Barrachs are still benefiting from quick and easy access to the mainland and from an improved air ambulance service now extended to all parts of Scotland. The carriage of urgent medical supplies, spare parts, newspapers and mail, which includes not a few purchases from home shopping catalogues, is expedited. Islanders working or studying away from home can travel to employment or higher education more quickly, while special fares mean that Barrachs can also make visits to relatives who have been airlifted to mainland hospitals. In a fragile economy based on crofting and fishing, and in which unemployment can fluctuate alarmingly, the income from summer tourism is invaluable. Visitors to the island are attracted by its scenic beauty, its history and its Gaelic culture. The existence of the air service enables travellers to fly into Barra quickly and easily, and this tourist traffic also brings additional revenue to the air service. The air link undoubtedly attracts some visitors who might otherwise be deterred by a long sea crossing and it also puts Barra within reach of those seeking only a short break from the pressures of city life. There can't be many who, at some time, have not had the overwhelming desire to drop everything and escape to a small island. Leisure traffic is two-way, however, and islanders have the world at their feet once they have reached Glasgow.

Travel is not all for pleasure. Much of it is necessary for those on duty or engaged in business. This might include supernumerary teachers, or an architect on local authority service, flying down from Stornoway or Benbecula; bank staff journeying to the mainland for a training course or flying in from the regional office.

Over 8,000 passengers use Barra airport annually. It doesn't make a profit but, as Barra hotelier and sometime Chairman of Western Isles Enterprise, George MacLeod, commented in a recent annual report of Highlands and Islands Airports Ltd, "A regular and affordable air service and airport for Barra is essential for our community." The air service provides an alternative to the ferry and, upon occasion, is able to operate when the ferry cannot.

The brief flurry of activity as the Twin Otter arrives and departs is soon replaced by the more natural sounds of the oyster-catcher with its black and white plumage, pink legs and orange-red bill. With the tide out, the casts of lugworms dot the beach and seabirds descend to feed. In the distance can be seen one or two islanders raking for cockles which, in times of hardship, once kept the island fed. As early as the sixteenth century it was noted that this was the place to come for the *cardium edule*. Following a tour of the islands in 1549, Donald Monro, High Dean of the Isles, wrote his Descriptione of the Western Iles of Scotland callit Hybrides in which he recorded, "...there is ane myle of braid sands quhilk ebbs ane myle, callit the Trayrmore of Kilbarry, that is, the Grate Sands of Barray. This sands is all full of grate cockills..."

The quiet on the surface belies the hive of activity which is taking place beneath. The bivalve molluscs, with the aid of a 'foot', bury themselves just deep enough to cover the shell and there they spend most of their time. Two short siphons project above the surface when the tide is in and one sucks in the water enabling the cockle to feed on microscopic plants. Following a short period recently, when mechanical harvesting of cockles was in vogue, a return to more traditional methods has been implemented as a conservation measure to combat declining stocks.

Another feature of the beach, until the closure of the business in 1996, was the occasional sight of a mechanical excavator removing cockle shell which was then dried and crushed at the Barra Shell plant, established in the mid-fifties at the former home of Compton Mackenzie. The final product, 'harl', has been used to good effect on the outside of the airport terminal building.

Soon the tide has turned, flowing through the Sound of Orosay and then slowly rippling across the flat, sandy expanse of the Tràigh Mhòr, cutting Orosay off until the next low water. The three barnacle-encrusted posts which indicate the seaward end of the 'runways' of the airport, are the only protrusions to break the vast expanse of water created by the high tide.

With the dispersal of passengers, 'meeters and greeters', and sightseers, the last of the sand will have been swept from the floor of the terminal waiting room to signal the end of another day at Barra Airport. It is a far cry from Heathrow, but then, that's the attraction. ✈

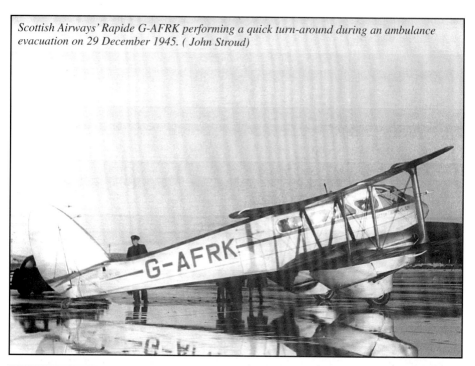

Scottish Airways' Rapide G-AFRK performing a quick turn-around during an ambulance evacuation on 29 December 1945. (John Stroud)

The BEA air terminal and the fire tender which was to disappear beneath the waves in 1968. (Photo courtesy of Tony Naylor)

BEA de Havilland Rapide G-AGIC taxies on the beach, c.1948. (Photo: A. A. MacGregor, courtesy of the Scottish Life Archive, National Museums of Scotland)

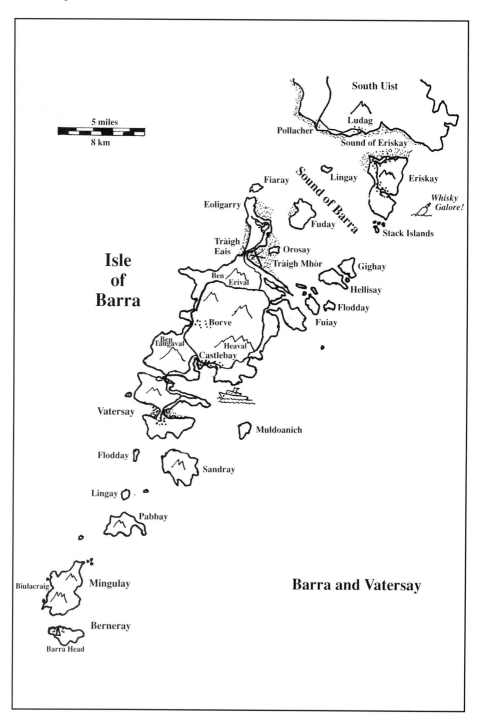

South Uist

Ludag

Pollacher

Sound of Eriskay

5 miles

8 km

Fiaray

Sound of Barra

Lingay

Eriskay

Whisky Galore!

Eoligarry

Fuday

Stack Islands

Tràigh Eais

Orosay

Tràigh Mhòr

Gighay

Isle of Barra

Ben Erival

Hellisay

Flodday

Borve

Fuiay

Ben Tangaval

Heaval

Castlebay

Vatersay

Muldoanich

Flodday

Sandray

Lingay

Pabbay

Biulacraig

Mingulay

Barra and Vatersay

Berneray

Barra Head

2

The Flightline to the Tideline

"Who needs an airfield when there are two broad miles of firm cockle-shell sand to land on?" Christopher Somerville in *The Other British Isles*, 1990.

In 1936, when the air service to Barra began, the island's roads were still unmetalled. The road from Northbay petered out at the side of the Tràigh Mhòr near Crannag, and horses, carts and the odd car, the first of which is believed to have arrived on Barra around 1926, had to cross the strand. A mile or so to the north, the road resumed its path across the machair to the Eoligarry school, then so recently built by Inverness County Council. Just over the hill lay Eoligarry House, once the home of the chiefs of the Clan MacNeil after they abandoned Kisimul Castle, and a few crofts on the peninsula so loved by the writer, Alasdair Alpin MacGregor. ("Ah! Eoligarry! The very name is mellifluous...")

Except for the school, the only building on the primrose covered neck of land linking Eoligarry to the rest of Barra, was Suidheachan, (pronounced "soo-yech-an") which Compton Mackenzie had built as his home. Constructed in 1935/36, the building materials were delivered directly to the Tràigh Mhòr by one of the many coal puffers which plied the waters of the west of Scotland.

Jimmy Orrell of Midland & Scottish Air Ferries landed on the Tràigh Mhòr, which MacGregor, in his romantic style, called the Great Cockle Shore, in 1933 while undertaking a search for landing sites in the islands. Although it pioneered the routes to Kintyre and Islay, that company never managed to start an air service to the Western Isles. Short Scion, G-ADDP, of West of Scotland Air Services, another airline which had ambitions to operate Hebridean air services, is recorded as landing on the beach during 1935. However the task of bringing such dreams to fruition fell to George Nicholson, who had formed Northern & Scottish Airways at Renfrew in 1934, and his Chief Pilot, David Barclay, with their introduction of regular air transport to Barra in 1936. There is little flat land on the island and, after their failure to find a suitable landing strip, it was the Northbay postmaster, John MacPherson, who asked Barclay if the beach could be used for such a service.

It was near Crannag that early pilots, such as Barclay, drew up the Spartan Cruisers and de Havilland Rapides (tide permitting) for the first ten years, and where a small hut was provided. Sometimes, however, the aircraft drew up further away, as happened to the author of a piece in *The Aeroplane* in July 1938 (and quoted in Peter Clegg's excellent history of Scottish Airways, *Wings over the Glens*), who was sampling the trip in unseasonable summer weather:

"At Barra we approached a wide, yellow beach, to leeward of a ridge which made itself felt in gusts. Barclay's landing was a work of art, and nearly full throttle was needed to taxi against the wind to where the car waited. The airport hut is slightly farther along the coast so the car had been brought to the machine... We dropped one passenger, an elderly lady, and took on two men. The crew crept into the car to fill in forms and sign manifests, etc. The Spartan rocked and the gale squealed over the cabin, although the motors were still running."

The Air Ministry officially licensed the Tràigh Mhòr as an airfield on 7 August 1936 although a few test landings had been undertaken earlier in the year and calls at Barra on demand had been offered since 10 June. A daily service to Barra was being promoted in the airline's advertisements in *The Oban Times* from early July although Barra was not included in the regular schedule, Glasgow-Skye-North Uist-Benbecula-South Uist-Barra-Glasgow and vice versa, until October. The airline's brochure *Go by Air* instructed intending passengers on Barra to contact 'John MacPherson, Post Office, North Bay'. The Coddy, as he was known, had added another job to the many responsibilities already held.

Although Northern & Scottish Airways had only been founded at Renfrew in late 1934, it had rapidly built up a considerable network. By the summer of 1936, it was also serving Tiree, Campbeltown, Islay, Harris, Belfast, the Isle of Man, Blackpool, Liverpool and Carlisle. Inverness-based Highland Airways and Northern & Scottish were now both part of the earlier British Airways group of companies, and one of these was subsequently allocated the Irish Sea services.

1936 saw Compton Mackenzie make his first journey by air. In *Octave 7* of his autobiography, he records writing to his wife, Faith, that "a Scottish Airways (sic) plane had taken Father MacKellaig, the Coddy, Neil Sinclair and myself to the South Uist Games; 8 minutes from the gates of *Suidheachan* to the grounds". The South Uist airfield was at Askernish and was served until 1939.

In October 1936, on his way to Barra, Mackenzie reached Glasgow and decided to take the flight rather than go by sea. This flight from Renfrew "...seemed more of an adventure. As we rose into the air, I thought that an airport which was not surrounded by a large cemetery would have been more reassuring to the novice." Arkleston Cemetery can still be seen today from the M8 motorway which passes over the site of Renfrew Airport.

Flying was considered by many to be daring and unsafe. Upon receiving a letter from Mackenzie about the trip from Renfrew to Barra, Calum MacSween replied, "I am afraid you may get a surprise some day. I have not much faith in motors. Even in a boat they are a risky business. To try one's life in the air is extremely so."

In August 1937, the British Airways group, in conjunction with the London Midland and Scottish Railway, and David MacBrayne Ltd, merged Northern & Scottish Airways with Inverness-based Highland Airways, to form a new company, Scottish Airways Ltd. British Airways held 50% of the share-holding of Scottish Airways Ltd while the LMSR controlled 40% and David MacBrayne Ltd 10%. Following the outbreak of war, Scottish Airways became part of the Associated Airways Joint Committee (AAJC) which was formed in 1940. Its Spartan Cruisers were requisitioned by the military but were soon disposed of, having become the victims of corrosion due to the beach landings at Barra. The Dragon Rapides were to soldier on for twenty years until 1955.

The circular road around Barra had been surfaced by 1939 following a protest inspired by Mackenzie and involving the withholding of the road tax. However, the road from Northbay to the Tràigh Mhòr was not included in the initial scheme and Mackenzie, in a 1943 article describing the hazards of a wartime journey by sea and rail from *Suidheachan* to London, memorably described it as "two miles of road likely to make a tank pensive."

The air service to and from Renfrew continued through part, if not all, of the war. Being in a military protected area, islanders needed permits to travel which, with wartime "red tape", were difficult to obtain. The windows of the Rapides were blacked out.

The event which would later provide the basis for one of Mackenzie's most famous books, took place off Eriskay in 1941 when the Harrison Line vessel, *SS Politician*, ran aground. Some of the whisky which was salvaged by islanders from Eriskay, South Uist and Barra is said to have found a ready market among the workers brought in to build the RAF airfield at Balivanich on Benbecula. Mackenzie wrote *Whisky Galore* after he left Barra in 1946 and Ealing Studios filmed it on location on Barra at the end of the summer of 1948.

It was Gabrielle Blunt's first film and the leading parts were played by Basil Radford, Joan Greenwood, James Robertson Justice, and Gordon Jackson. Still 'treading the boards' and appearing in television drama, Gabrielle remembers being pictured at Tràigh Mhòr meeting Gordon Jackson arriving on the aircraft from Glasgow, having travelled from Australia to take part in the film. They were to stay in a house at Breivig during the shooting of the film. She retains fond memories of the flights from Renfrew in the Rapide, "I felt very safe in them. You felt that, if the engine failed, you'd land gently, like a moth. And the pilots were brilliant." Gabrielle Blunt and Joan Greenwood, who played the Macroon sisters in the film, walked round the island when they were not required for filming. Gabrielle recalls stopping at Northbay where, "the Coddy gave us each a wee dram of the real contraband whisky to help us on our way".

John MacPherson, already sixty when air services began, retired just after the war and was initially succeeded by his son, Angus, who was back from war service. The post-war Labour Government of 1945 included air transport in its nationalisation plans and thus Scottish Airways was absorbed by the new state air corporation, British European Airways, in February 1947. The original hut at the south side of the Tràigh Mhòr was replaced by a new one near the site of today's passenger terminal.

One of the Rapide aircraft, G-AGJF, was written off after an incident on the Tràigh Mhòr on 6 August 1947. It is believed that it may have sunk in soft sand and then been caught by the incoming tide. It was later hauled off the beach and burnt.

Angus MacPherson's sister, Katie, took over the job of Station Superintendent about 1950, having previously worked in a children's home in England before returning to the island initially to run the shop at Northbay for her father.

There is only one incident in which injury is known to have been caused to passengers at the Tràigh Mhòr. This involved BEA Dragon Rapide G-AGPH while it was on air ambulance duty on the morning of 6 December 1951. During its landing at Barra, the aircraft wheels stuck in soft sand resulting in its turning over to come to rest upside down. Both of the two elderly female passengers on board, en route to their homes in North Uist following hospital confinements in Glasgow, suffered shock, cuts and bruises. Sadly, 81-year-old Mrs McKillop of Lochportain, died at home a day later.

The de Havilland DH89 Rapides had been the workhorses of the air for many years. Aviation writer, John Stroud, records that "the type did more than any other to establish UK air services". However, with the exception of scheduled services to Tiree and Barra, and Scotland-wide air ambulance operations, BEA's Rapides had all been withdrawn from Scottish services by 1952 and the search was on for an aircraft with a fixed undercarriage suitable for flights in and out of the Tràigh Mhòr. The airline had evaluated a Heron aircraft, also from de Havilland, on routes to the Channel Islands in 1951 and it was decided to order two Series 1B for services in Scotland.

The two new aircraft were delivered in February 1955 - coincidentally the month in which John MacPherson died - and scheduled operations by the four-engine Herons to Barra began in mid-April. Apart from being able to carry more passengers than the Rapide bi-plane, they looked very modern in comparison and must have come as a revelation to the islanders. Apart from anything else, the new undercarriage layout meant that passengers no longer had to climb a gradient to take their seats upon boarding the aircraft.

In a naming ceremony at Renfrew Airport, performed by Jean Jolly, matron at Glasgow's Southern General Hospital, G-ANXA was named *Sir John Hunter* and G-ANXB, *Sir James Simpson*. The latter was subsequently adjusted to *Sir James Young Simpson*. A third Heron, G-AOFY, *Sir Charles Bell*, was delivered in 1956. This aircraft was subsequently lost in the air ambulance crash at Islay on 28 September 1957. As a consequence, G-ANXA was renamed *Sister Jean Kennedy* in honour of the nurse who died in the tragic accident.

Scottish Airways had included Barra in a circular Skye and Western Isles service before the war but, in BEA days, Barra was usually served from Glasgow via Tiree. Five or six flights a week operated but, in winter, more often than not, only three extended beyond Tiree.

David Barclay, who had inaugurated services in 1936 as Chief Pilot with Northern & Scottish Airways, eventually retired from BEA in 1965 having spent almost his whole career flying around Scotland. The following year, Abbotsinch replaced Renfrew as the airport for Glasgow. Renfrew's runway would later disappear under the carriageways of the M8 motorway and beneath streets of new housing with names recalling the types of aircraft which once used the airfield and some of the islands served. Thus there is both a *Heron Way* and a *Barra Avenue*. Renfrew's 1954 passenger terminal was demolished in 1977, having lain empty for nearly as long as it was in use, and was replaced by a supermarket.

Katie MacPherson continued in charge at Barra throughout the remaining life of British European Airways and beyond. Other islanders were employed to operate the fire vehicle and to carry out such duties as baggage handling. Donald Sinclair and Donald Campbell became long serving employees. A larger hut was eventually supplied - across the road from today's terminal. The all-weather road around the shore, avoiding the need to reach Eoligarry by crossing the strand, was completed in 1960.

BEA's fleet almost suffered a fifty percent reduction when G-ANXA *Sister Jean Kennedy* stuck fast at Tràigh Mhòr on 30 March 1968 and remained so in the face of the incoming tide. Captain Andy Guthrie and Captain Peter Morgan had brought the aircraft into Barra at 1115 hours. They boarded the returning passengers and the take-off checks were carried out on the move so as to avoid coming to a halt anywhere on the lower part of the beach. Peter Morgan describes what happened next, "Captain Guthrie turned the aircraft quite tightly, left-handed into the wind and the aircraft came to a stop. At first I thought that he was concerned with the direction or strength of the wind. He then opened the engines to full power but we still did not move. I glanced across to see that he was not using the thumb brakes. Almost instantaneously, I became aware that we were settling gently to port. I shall never forget the look of horror on his face as the same realisation dawned on him. I then ripped off my safety harness and sprinted past the startled passengers, out of the door and round to the front of the port wing. By the time that I got there, the No. 1 (port outer) propeller was within about an inch of the surface of the sand and I had no alternative but to give the pilot the "cut" signal to close down the engines. In retrospect, I think it was a good thing that we did this promptly as, apart from the risk of damage to the propeller and engine, the vibration was definitely hastening our descent. We then called Kitty on the radio and she dispatched Donald Sinclair and Donald Campbell with the fire truck. As it arrived, it too settled rapidly until it bellied in a patch of sand that was literally quaking around them as they got out of the vehicle."

The rescue attempt was carried out in the presence of a reporter and photographer from the *Daily Record*, who had been passengers on the incoming flight. Peter Morgan continues, "Various attempts were made to extract the aircraft using the passengers and several locals. Initially this was unsuccessful, but with the aid of some planks, two tractors from the shell-grit firm, and a lot of digging, heaving and swearing, she came out of her hole. At this moment, Captain Guthrie was up at the hut trying to get some inspiration from Glasgow. I therefore leapt into the cockpit to start her up and taxi up the beach away from the tide, now only twenty yards away. At this moment, the main starter solenoid decided to fail and we were left with no power and a diminishing amount of air pressure in the brake system which left us with limited steering. Eventually she was towed up the beach behind one of the tractors, with Captain Guthrie desperately trying to keep her straight and hoping that there would be enough pressure left to stop him running into the tractor when they got to the hut. We then made efforts to extract the fire truck but without success. It was much heavier and much more deeply embedded than 'XA had been. With the tide lapping around our feet, we lashed forty gallon drums around it and retreated up the beach with a long piece of rope."

BEA's Glasgow base dispatched the other Heron aircraft, G-ANXB, to Barra with the Station Engineer, Jock McAvoy, and Captain Ian Montgomery to assist with repairs to 'XA. With the tide rising rapidly, G-ANXB landed on the beach much later than would have normally been thought wise. 'XA's crew, who had been delayed for around six hours, returned with 'XB. Meanwhile, on Barra, the race against time and tide

Jimmy Orrell of Midland & Scottish Air Ferries made the first visit by air to Barra when, on 14 June 1933, he landed Dragon G-ACCZ on the Tràigh Mhòr. Here, sister aircraft, G-ACDL, is seen at Campbeltown to which Midland & Scottish had begun Scotland's first scheduled air service two months earlier. (Courtesy of Catherine Cameron)

West of Scotland Air Services' Short Scion G-ADDP on the Tràigh Mhòr during 1935. (Courtesy of Mary Catherine Maclean, Barra Heritage Centre)

Heave ... and the battle to free the Heron is on. The Heron was eventually released from the entrapping sands before she was reached by the incoming tide on 30 March 1968. Barra's fire tender was not so fortunate. (Photo by Robert Hotchkiss courtesy of Mirror Syndication International)

British Airways Scottish Division Shorts Skyliner at its Glasgow base in August 1973. (Wilf White)

continued. In its story, captioned 'The Sea Shall Not Have Her', BEA News reported, "After temporary repairs to the slightly damaged port undercarriage were made by the Station Engineer, the Heron was ready to fly."

"But her four engines would not start," the article continues. "For a frantic forty minutes, the engineer undertook the back breaking job of turning the propellers by hand." Heron 'XA finally departed from the Tràigh Mhòr. This was undoubtedly to the relief of BEA's Glasgow base. In the past there had been occasions when aircraft had become slightly bogged down in wet sand but this incident had coincided with one of the highest tides of the year. The fire truck was hauled to dry land at the next low tide, *BEA News* reporting that it was being sent to Glasgow "for repair".

BEA's fleet in Scotland, the Herons and the Viscounts, acquired new *BEA Scottish Airways* titles in 1971 which happily recalled earlier times. The Civil Aviation Act of that year led to the merger of BEA and BOAC between 1972 and 1974 and the end was also in sight for the de Havilland Herons. They were both withdrawn in March 1973 after eighteen years of sterling service to Barra.

At the end of 1972, Loganair was entrusted with conveying the body of Sir Compton Mackenzie to Barra for burial. He had requested that he be laid to rest in the cemetery at Cille Bharra alongside such friends as John MacPherson. About one hundred people met the special Shorts Skyvan charter flight on 4 December when it landed on the Tràigh Mhòr in atrocious weather conditions.

British Airways brought two Shorts Skyliners, a development of the Skyvan, into service to replace the Herons. BEA's first choice for a Heron replacement had been the Britten-Norman Trislander but because of the manufacturer's internal problems at that time, it was temporarily unavailable. The contract therefore went to Shorts of Belfast for their SC7 Skyliner. These cuboid-looking aircraft were unsuitable as air ambulances, because of their higher operating cost, and British Airways relinquished the contract which was subsequently awarded to Loganair. This small Scottish airline had been founded in 1962 as an air taxi operator, but by the early seventies was expanding its network of scheduled services. British Airways wished to divest itself of its thinner routes and the Glasgow-Tiree-Barra service was subcontracted to Loganair in October 1974. Loganair took over the service entirely in 1975. Since then the service was continuously subsidised by the Scottish Office until 1999 when this responsibility passed to the Scottish Executive. The aircraft used was the three-engined Isle of Wight-built Trislander, which BEA had earlier planned to purchase and itself a development of the Britten-Norman Islander. Katie MacPherson remained with Loganair until ill-health forced her to retire in 1980.

With local government re-organisation in 1975, Comhairle nan Eilean, the Western Isles Islands Council, was created. The new authority decided to subsidise a new Western Isles inter-island service linking Stornoway, Benbecula and Barra, and a Loganair Islander aircraft launched the service in the autumn of that year. Since then, the route, together with a growing number of car ferries, bridges and causeways, has helped to link together the southern isles of Barra and the Uists with Harris and Lewis.

During the winter of 1976/7, the inter-island air service operated to Barra three times weekly. During the same period, the service from Glasgow to Barra, via Tiree, was offered on Mondays, Wednesdays, Fridays and Saturdays. In the summer of 1977, however, the Glasgow-Barra service operated non-stop daily, including Sundays, between 15 May and 2 October. Daily except Sunday operation is now the normal pattern on the Glasgow route in both summer and winter.

The present passenger terminal building at Barra was opened by Loganair in 1978 during the period when the airline was owned by the Royal Bank of Scotland. Loganair's operation of the terminal was emphasised by a large representation of the airline's logo on the front of the building. The Terminal and the Tràigh Mhòr, featured in an unusual 1989 film, *Play me Something*, described as, "a man entertaining passengers waiting at Barra Airport with a tale of an Italian peasant on a trip to Venice". A Twin Otter aircraft also makes a brief appearance in the 1994 production, *Staggered*.

Female management of the airport continued right up until 1994. Initially Katie MacPherson had been succeeded by a niece, Una, while another niece, Elizabeth had relieved Katie periodically. Una was followed by Eona Macleod. In March 1984, Janet MacLean took up the post and, although the airport is no longer in Loganair's hands, Janet is still with Loganair today as the airline's Station Manager at Barra.

The Islander and Trislander aircraft were replaced by the rugged Canadian-built Twin Otters in the early nineteen-eighties, most of which were delivered by Loganair pilots directly from the de Havilland Canada factory in Ontario. Apart from a less than successful experiment with the larger Shorts 360 in the summer of 1994, of which more later, the Twin Otter still serves Barra well today. In view of the need to increase fire safety cover, the management and operation of the airport was given up by Loganair in April 1994. It is now in the hands of Highlands and Islands Airports Ltd, founded in 1986 and, since July 1999, owned by the First Minister.

In 1987, both Loganair and Manx Airlines became part of Airlines of Britain Holdings. The major constituent of this group was British Midland Airways which grew to include Manx Airlines Europe (now renamed British Regional Airlines) and Business Air. While remaining a separate entity within the group, Loganair became a franchisee of British Airways and from 11 July 1994 assumed all operations as British Airways Express. In return for a fee, British Airways provides yield management (the art of maximising revenue), marketing and sales services.

After a fifteen year period, during which Loganair had grown considerably with many scheduled services into England and as far south as Jersey in the Channel Islands, a 1994 reorganisation within the group led to operations being restricted mostly to Scotland. Further changes at Airlines of Britain Holdings in 1996 led to the demerger of the group with British Midland becoming separate from a new British Regional Airlines (Holdings) Group which incorporated British Regional Airlines, Business Air, Loganair, and Manx Airlines. The culmination for Loganair was a successful management buy-out in March 1997 led by Scott Grier OBE who became chairman of Loganair. Following a progressive return of routes from British Regional Airlines, the Loganair network, after two years, incorporated Barra, Benbecula, Campbeltown, Edinburgh, Glasgow, Inverness, Islay, Londonderry, Tiree, and Wick, plus internal networks within Orkney and Shetland. The Loganair fleet (July 1999) consists of five Shorts 360s, one DHC6 Twin Otter, five Britten-Norman BN2B Islanders and two Saab SF340B aircraft.

The provision of a hard runway has exercised the Council considerably during the mid-nineties. In 1993, Comhairle nan Eilean commissioned a feasibility report on the subject and in 1996 made the issue the subject of a non-binding referendum on the island. The proposals are covered in Chapter 6.

In 1995, the inter-island service linking Stornoway, Benbecula and Barra had been put out to tender by Comhairle nan Eilean. Several companies sought information but, in the end, Loganair was the only company to put in a bid. The route was later divided, British Regional Airlines operating the Stornoway-Benbecula sector with the Shorts 360, while Loganair's Twin Otter schedule was dovetailed to provide through connections between Barra and Benbecula. The Barra-Benbecula sector was subcontracted to Loganair by BRAL. British Regional Airlines subsequently decided to phase out operation of the Shorts 360 and, in early 1998, intimated its decision not to submit a bid when the tender became due for renewal that summer. Loganair was the only airline to bid and it was awarded the new contract.

It would appear, however, that operations on the beach are set to continue for some time. Soon after Highlands and Islands Airports Ltd took over operation of the airport, the Eoligarry Airport Consultative Committee was established to ensure that the airport is a good neighbour to the community. During 1996, a 'one-off' charter operated from Barra to give islanders and visitors a look at St. Kilda from the air. Regrettably, visibility was not at its best on this occasion, but it would seem to be the type of opportunity which Loganair might look at again in the future when it is not so reliant on one aircraft at Barra. Sightseeing trips were previously flown by Loganair during the early years of its operations at Barra.

Loganair has been interested in acquiring a second Twin Otter but, to date, a suitable example has not been identified. This would provide back-up for the Twin Otter-operated routes should G-BVVK be out of service for any reason. The only other Twin Otter operating scheduled services in the UK is G-BIHO of Isles of Scilly Skybus. This aircraft has been operated by Loganair on short-term leases to relieve 'Victor Kilo'.

The socially necessary air service between Glasgow and Barra is subsidised by the Scottish Executive under the provisions of the Highlands and Islands Air Services (Scotland) Act of 1980. The service could not be provided on a commercial basis and subsidy is made available to meet the deficit incurred. Maintenance of a scheduled service between the mainland and a small island such as Barra is "essential to counter the island's peripherality, fragile economic base and depopulation."

Barra and Vatersay are remote. Access to a major service centre such as Glasgow for financial, professional, health and other services which cannot be provided locally is essential for the maintenance of the economic and social fabric of the area. Current European Union rules on the single market with regard to aviation mean that a Public Service Obligation (PSO) can be imposed on a route serving a peripheral region in order to protect a service which would not be offered commercially. PSOs have been imposed on both the Glasgow-Barra and Glasgow-Tiree routes. The current three year contract expires on 31 March 2000. I was advised by the Scottish Office Development Department in June 1998 that the tender price for the 1998/99 financial year for these two routes is £175,800.

Loganair's Station Manager at Barra, Janet MacLean, has two relief members of staff, while Highlands and Islands Airports Ltd at Barra Airport now employs six people as ramp handlers/firefighters and one administration officer. Sub Officer/Manager is Michael Galbraith who replaced Keith Rendall in late 1998. Traffic levels at Barra have changed little in recent years although there was an identifiable increase in 1989/90 during the construction of the Vatersay causeway. In a bid to stimulate tourist traffic, Loganair recently joined with rail and ferry companies to offer short holiday breaks to Barra which combine rail and sea travel in one direction with a flight in the Twin Otter.

Arrivals at Tràigh Mhòr are now overseen from the new tower and lookout deck, built in 1997. This also incorporates extended facilities for the firefighters and, at the same time, some internal remodelling of the terminal, which included provision for disabled access, was undertaken.

Now that the continuing story of Barra Airport has been brought through the last six decades, the following chapters look at other aspects of the story since 1936. ✈

Spartan Cruiser II, G-ACSM of Scottish Airways was a regular visitor until impressed into RAF service in April 1940. The RAF discovered that Barra operations had caused serious corrosion and it was withdrawn three months later. (John Stroud)

Joan Greenwood arrives for the filming of Whisky Galore! (Canal + Image UK)

G-ANXB made the first Heron training flight to Barra on 20 March 1955. The crew line-up is S/A J. D. Tweddle, Captain D. Jack, Captain W. St. C. Reid, Captain W. C. Yorston, R/O A. Edmiston, and Captain David Barclay. (Photo: BEA, courtesy of Joe Tweddle)

3

Tràigh Mhòr Snapshots

"...the only thing I miss about flying is flying around the Scottish islands." The late Captain Eric Starling quoted in his biography, *The Flight of the Starling* by Iain Hutchison, 1992.

Barra Airport and its air service have seen the involvement of many people during six decades. Some of those have earned a special place in the evolution of the Tràigh Mhòr. Its biggest personality, in every sense of the word, was not connected with the air service, but it would seem a great oversight not to include Sir Compton Mackenzie, the author of *Whisky Galore*.

George Nicholson - Airline Entrepreneur

Born in Consett, Co. Durham, in 1905, George Nicholson founded Northern Airways at Cramlington Airfield, Northumberland, in July, 1934. In November 1934, he relocated to Renfrew and his airline became Northern & Scottish Airways Ltd. As we have seen, the Company inaugurated services to Barra in the summer of 1936. Having already taken over services previously operated by Midland & Scottish Air Ferries to Kintyre and Islay, it also introduced flights to Skye, South Uist, Benbecula, North Uist and Harris. To Nicholson, therefore, goes the credit of linking the Outer Hebrides by air to the mainland and introducing all the advantages which air travel has brought to these islands over the decades.

The network of routes across Scotland which were pioneered by George Nicholson's airline, along with Edmund Fresson's Highland Airways, Eric Gandar Dower's Allied Airways and John Sword's Midland & Scottish Air Ferries, is still largely the same as that flown today by British Regional Airlines and Loganair. Nicholson accompanied his Chief Pilot, David Barclay, on many trips to negotiate the development of the airfields around his network and he managed Scottish Airways' southern base at Renfrew following the merger between Northern & Scottish Airways and Highland Airways in 1937. He was made redundant by BEA in 1948 following the nationalisation of the private airlines the previous year. George Nicholson died in South Africa in 1950.

David Barclay - Loyal Service to the Islands

David Barclay was born in Greenock in 1905, the son of a dairyman. Following service in the Royal Air Force, he spent virtually his whole career flying around Scotland. By the time he retired in 1965 at the age of 60, he had been landing on the Tràigh Mhòr for thirty years.

He was appointed Chief Pilot of Northern & Scottish Airways in 1935 as the network of scheduled services throughout the Hebrides was established. Awarded the MBE in 1944, David Barclay made a major contribution to air transport in Scotland during his long flying career which continued with Scottish Airways and BEA. In addition to flying scheduled services, he operated 1,271 air ambulance flights.

The people of Barra turned out in force to recognise this contribution when David Barclay flew there in command of BEA Heron G-ANXB, his last visit prior to retiral on 30 April 1965. The BEA house magazine carried a picture on its front cover of the crowd which assembled on the beach. Noting that Barclay had logged 1.5 million miles in his 18,000 hours in the air, mostly over the short Highlands and Islands air routes, the magazine gave a detailed report of his final flight:

"It was a clear day, and all eyes gazed into the brilliant blue sky to catch the first glimpse of the aircraft approaching over the sea. A shout went up as a speck appeared in the sky - the signal also for piper Callum Johnston to play his welcome as the aircraft made a circuit of the beach and then touched gently down. As it taxied in, the islanders, led by the piper, walked along the beach to the aircraft giving a tremendous cheer as David opened the aircraft door. There were speeches, presentations (including one of cockles), pats on the back, reminiscences, but above all the noise could be heard the skirling of the pipes, the gaiety of the Scottish music having a counter melody of sadness on this occasion. It was one huge happy family gathering to pay tribute to one of its sons. Like the best of parties, it had to end. David gathered the ship's papers from Kitty MacPherson, BEA Station Superintendent, Barra, and followed by the islanders, was piped along the beach to the aircraft. He mounted the aircraft steps, turned to the crowd and, cap in hand, raised his arms in salute. The beach was cleared for take-off and once airborne, the aircraft banked to make a final run in over the islanders, dipping its wings in salute - a last farewell from Captain Barclay before disappearing over the sea."

David Barclay's daughter, a BEA stewardess, accompanied him that day and further celebrations were awaiting him when G-ANXB landed back at Renfrew. Following the closure of Renfrew Airport in 1966, it was David Barclay who was invited to unveil the Royal Burgh of Renfrew's air ambulance memorial. David Barclay died in 1981.

Although never directly associated with Loganair, it was this airline which named a number of aircraft after him at different times. The tradition continues today with G-BPCA, a Britten-Norman Islander in Scottish Ambulance Service livery, named in his honour.

John MacPherson - Businessman and Seanachaidh

Soon after regular flights to Barra began, it was John MacPherson who was appointed as the local agent on Barra for Northern & Scottish Airways. Born on 26 December 1876 on a croft at Buaile nam Bodach, Barra, some 25 years before the Wright Brothers made the first power-sustained flight in the USA, he was appointed Postmaster at Northbay in 1923. Nicknamed *The Coddy*, he was a renowned Gaelic folklorist and a good friend of Compton Mackenzie during the writer's residence on the island. *Tales from Barra told by The Coddy*, first published posthumously in 1960, reappeared in print in 1992. He was an Inverness County Councillor for the north end of Barra, he ran a croft and a guest house, and he was the owner of one of the first cars on the island. He can be seen in a scene in the film, *Whisky Galore!* During filming at the end of the wet summer of 1948, MacPherson became the "transportation captain" for Ealing Studios throughout its presence on the island. The MacPhersons maintained a remarkable and lengthy connection with the airport as John was succeeded upon his retiral by his son, Angus, and then by his daughter, Catherine (Katie). After Katie's stint of nearly thirty years, she was followed briefly by her niece, Una MacPherson. John MacPherson died in 1955.

Katie MacPherson - Station Superintendent

Katie MacPherson was BEA's Station Manager at Barra from 1951 until 1974, followed by a short spell with British Airways before transferring to Loganair until 1980 when ill health forced her into retirement (and direct experience of the air ambulance). She would be amazed at the number of people involved in the running of the airport today, having performed the role with little assistance for so many years. Female airport managers are no more common today. Ms Lesley Bale, now at Edinburgh Airport, was the only one in western Europe when she took up her previous post at Aberdeen Airport, and remained so until Janis Kong assumed the position of Managing Director of London Gatwick in April 1997. In the early BEA days, Katie was given a small hand-held walkie-talkie radio to communicate with incoming pilots. She took bookings and issued tickets, made up the aircraft load sheets, and gave the pilots weather reports. During the summer, she ran a guest house and she was on call at any time should an island doctor request an air ambulance charter. Katie was awarded the MBE in 1969 and was a recipient of the *Woman of the Year* award.

Eric Starling - Pioneer Aviator and Flight Manager

Eric Starling was born in London in 1911. His early career was as Chief Pilot with Aberdeen-based Allied Airways (Gandar Dower) Ltd during which he launched scheduled services to Shetland, and, the first scheduled air service across the North Sea, between Newcastle and Stavanger. He joined Scottish Airways in 1946 and was soon flying services to the Western Isles and Belfast. He recorded his first landing on the Tràigh Mhòr on 23 October 1946. During a long career with British European Airways at Renfrew and Abbotsinch from 1947 until 1971, he had a close association with the Scottish Air Ambulance Service. Just before to his retiral, he celebrated the 40th anniversary of his first solo flight in 1931 with a Barra roster. His pleasure in flying around Scotland was in getting away from the controlled airways "to places like Barra, and splashing down on the sands, winds and tides permitting, and hearing Kitty MacPherson's delightful voice over the walkie-talkie she used for communicating with us." Eric was hosted by Loganair on a short visit to Barra and Benbecula in January 1997, his first return visit since his retiral. Eric Starling died in November 1997 at the age of 85.

Sir Compton Mackenzie - Novelist

Sir Compton Mackenzie died in Edinburgh on 30 November 1972. He had made it known that he wished to be laid to rest on Barra and Loganair's Chief Pilot, Ken Foster, was at the controls of the Shorts Skyvan which had been chartered to carry his coffin and a party of family and friends to the island. Ken Foster reveals in an article in *The Scots Magazine* that lack of navigational aids at Barra, combined with poor visibility and gale force winds which changed direction, caused the aircraft to "miss" the island. This only came to light when the crew recognised Barra Head Lighthouse on the southernmost island of Berneray. After a change of course, the aircraft was soon splashing down on the Tràigh Mhòr where a crowd was waiting despite the grim weather. Eighty-two year old Callum Johnston played the pipes as the coffin was removed from the aircraft. It was transferred to the minibus, which served as the island's ambulance, for the two mile journey to the cemetery at Cille Bharra. A sombre occasion, it became even sadder when Callum Johnston collapsed and died after playing once more at the cemetery.

Compton Mackenzie lived on Barra from 1933 until 1946, first in rented accommodation and then in his own home, *Suidheachan*. For over a decade, the great and famous flocked there to visit Mackenzie. Born in 1883 to theatrical parents, Compton Mackenzie was a prodigious writer who had a habit of getting up very late in the day and writing all night. A founder of the *Sea League* which campaigned for protection of local fishing rights in the Minch, he became a convert to Roman Catholicism and had been described as a "professional Scot". He co-founded the magazine, *The Gramophone*, but he was perennially short of money. Considering his extensive literary output, it is ironic that he is best remembered for *Whisky Galore* and no doubt Sandy Mackendrick's film has much to do with this. A man who obviously thought a lot of himself, (his autobiography runs to eight volumes) he had a cameo role in the Ealing Studios film, as the Captain of the *SS Cabinet Minister*, a depiction of the *SS Politician*, the ship loaded with whisky which ran aground off Eriskay. Following his departure from Barra in 1946, he lived for a time in the south of England before moving to Edinburgh in 1953 for the last two decades of his life. "Mackenzie", said Katie MacPherson, "fitted perfectly into the classless society of our island".

Janet MacLean and Jane Colledge - Today's Airline Agents

In recent years, Janet MacLean, and her relief, Jane Colledge, have been the human face of Loganair on Barra. Janet initially took the job in 1984 for a six month period. She smiles when she tells you that she has now been doing it for fifteen years. Born in Kent, her father is from Eriskay and her mother is from Barra. Previously employed in the hotel trade, Janet is married with two children. She has direct experience of the air ambulance, having been airlifted at short notice from the Tràigh Mhòr one night in April 1994 for the birth of one of her children. In addition to undertaking regular passenger service duties, Janet and Jane have to file hourly weather reports to the Met Office between 9.00am and 4.00pm. Jane relieves Janet for days off and holidays, while a second relief, Janette Macdonald, can be called upon if neither Janet nor Jane are available. Jane Colledge was interviewed by ex-Beirut hostage John McCarthy in 1994 for the BBC television *Island Race* series.

Keith Rendall - The Orcadian

Keith Rendall was born on the low-lying Orkney island of Sanday, the largest of the north isles of Orkney. Sanday's association with Loganair is even longer than that of Barra, the airline's inaugural flight of the Orkney internal air service taking place between Kirkwall and Sanday on 27 September 1967. Keith moved to the Orkney capital, Kirkwall, at the age of thirteen and after training as an agricultural engineer, he joined Highlands and Islands Airports at Kirkwall Airport in August 1989. This "Gruellie Belkie", as natives of Sanday are called, relocated to Barra in November 1994. Keith loved working at Barra Airport although he occasionally hankered after the high life of Kirkwall, claiming to miss "wide roads, Sunday papers on Sunday, fast food and B & Q". There are not many airports that are also tourist attractions. With the islanders also very proud of their airport, Keith felt honoured to be running it. For four years he was senior firefighter and the first manager of the airport under HIAL operation. Keith was succeeded by local man, Michael Galbraith, following his return to Kirkwall in 1998. ✈

BEA's de Havilland Heron G-ANXB
passes above Katie MacPherson, walkie-talkie in hand.
(BEA photo courtesy of Tony Naylor)

Loganair Britten-Norman Islander G-BLNW operating on behalf of the Scottish Ambulance Service. (Photo by the author)

Patient transfer from home to aircraft. (Photo by the author)

▼ *Marginal ambulance operation - one wheel in the water. (H. E. Couzens)*

4

The Air Ambulance

"The regular passenger flights always landed at low tide but, on ambulance flights, we sometimes had to touch down in a few inches of water. Welly boots were an integral part of my equipment on those occasions." Nurse Lesley Crawford, quoted in *Air Ambulance* by Iain Hutchison, 1996.

Ever since Midland & Scottish Air Ferries was asked to fly a patient from Islay to Renfrew in May 1933, the airlines serving the Hebrides have been carrying patients to hospital. Indeed, one of the earliest flights by Northern & Scottish Airways to Barra in 1936 was at the request of a local doctor for the evacuation of a patient to hospital. In those pre-National Health Service days, patients who were able, had to re-imburse the County Council for the cost of the flight.

For many years the service was operated under contract by BEA, and later Loganair, to the Scottish Home and Health Department. Nowadays the service is organised by the Scottish Ambulance Service NHS Trust with the flying shared between Bond Aviation and Loganair. The service carried approximately 2,000 patients during 1994.

The death in Shetland of Loganair pilot, Captain Alan Young, on 20 May 1996 while on air ambulance duty was a timely reminder of the debt we owe to the personnel who provide this service.

As mentioned briefly in Chapter Two, an accident befell an aircraft on air ambulance duty to Barra in 1951. The morning of 6 December had already seen one air ambulance flight leave the Tràigh Mhòr to take two children to Glasgow. This had been followed by the usual service 'plane. A short time later, DH89 Dragon Rapide G-AGPH approached from Glasgow, en route to North Uist where it was to uplift another patient. The aircraft was also returning two elderly patients, who had been in Glasgow hospitals, to North Uist.

On landing at the Tràigh Mhòr, the aircraft's undercarriage stuck fast in soft sand and, as a result, the aircraft overturned. On board was the pilot, radio officer, Nurse Whelan and the two patients. Castlebay's district nurse, Catherine Macdougall, happened to be driving to the airport and witnessed the accident. When she reached the aircraft, she was able to assist the pilot and nurse in removing one patient, 81-year-old Mrs McKillop, through a hole in the aircraft. Staff of Hebridean Shell Grit (the operation which preceded Barra Shell), who had been working on the beach, were also quickly on the scene and they helped the other casualties from the aircraft. This involved some urgency as the fast incoming tide had already surrounded the aircraft. The pilot was bleeding badly and the young radio officer was suffering from shock. The second patient was suffering from cuts and bruising. Both patients were taken to a nearby house where they were kept warm and given medical attention.

Next day, Captain David Barclay flew to Barra in another Rapide and left two engineers to inspect the damaged aircraft. He flew on to North Uist with the two patients from the stricken aircraft, subsequently joined by Mrs McKillop's daughter who had travelled from Glasgow. Sadly, the episode ended with the death of Mrs McKillop at her home. For Nurse Whelan, on her first trip to the Hebrides, it was an unfortunate introduction. And for Rapide G-AGPH, it was the end of the line, as the aircraft was written off by BEA.

Barra's beach airstrip and the activities of the air ambulance service often combined to attract the attention of journalists. The work of the air ambulance service featured in such publications as *Picture Post* (June 1947), *Meccano Magazine* (March 1959), the BEA house magazine, a BEA documentary film... and continues to gain coverage in contemporary media. No longer do patients have to suffer the indignity of being delivered to the strand on the back of a lorry, as appears to have been the case in the 1947 photographs.

Although it is sudden emergencies and inflight births which make news headlines, much of the work of the service involves moving patients for non-emergency treatment. Ambulance flights from the Isle of Barra are normally heading for Glasgow and its big hospitals, to Raigmore Hospital in Inverness, or more recently, to the new 200-plus bed Ospadal nan Eilean / Western Isles Hospital in Stornoway.

If the local GP decides that an evacuation is necessary, he currently calls the 24-hour Air Desk at Aberdeen where arrangements for the flight are coordinated. It is usually the local doctor who decides to which hospital the patient is to be sent. After the initial 1993 reorganisation of the service, the Western Isles were dependent upon the helicopters at Plockton, Inverness or Prestwick. However, dissatisfaction with their non-availability during the hours of darkness, and their lack of space for accompanying family members, led to Loganair being requested to reopen its Air Ambulance Unit at Glasgow, in addition to the dedicated ambulance aircraft which it maintained for the service in Orkney and Shetland.

Since November 1993, Loganair's Britten-Norman Islander aircraft G-BPCA and G-BLNW, painted in the gaudy yellow colours of the Scottish Ambulance Service, have become familiar and re-assuring sights on the Tràigh Mhòr. The short take-off and landing capabilities of this aircraft type make it ideal for reaching the smallest of airstrips. The skills of the pilots mean that even with a high tide, the aircraft will still land at Barra to uplift a patient in an emergency.

Expectant mothers are often taken off the island by the air ambulance, to give birth in one of the specialist maternity units, as scheduled flights cannot carry expectant mothers beyond the end of the 38th week of their pregnancy. During the period of BEA's operation of the service, two mothers from Barra gave birth inflight. Although Loganair has now recorded 21 inflight births since 1973, and there have been eight from the more populous Isle of Islay, none have been on flights from the Tràigh Mhòr - yet!

The story of the air ambulance service inevitably involves tragic personal circumstances when seriously ill patients do not recover to return to their island homes. Equally, it has generated many amusing tales, such as the Rapide aircraft used to chase a bullock from the beach, and the plight of young nurses who suffered from air sickness while trying to tend their patients. ✈

Heron G-ANXA makes an idyllic scene complete in 1958. (J. F. MacN. Partridge)

In the days before Loganair's scheduled network extended to Barra, aircraft such as this Britten-Norman Islander in 1970 called regularly on charter assignments. (Bob Armstrong)

De Havilland Dove G-AWPH, 7 September 1971, during one of its regular visits to collect a cargo of lobsters. (Phil Lo Bao)

Peregrine Air Services' Piper Twin Commanche, to which the photographer's daughter Sally took a shine, was also a 1971 visitor carrying executives of the shell extraction company. (Bob Armstrong)

The Loganair terminal in 1989. (Photo by the author)

Terminal and control tower operated by Highlands and Islands Airports Ltd. (H. E. Couzens)

Loganair inaugurated scheduled services between Glasgow and Barra with the Britten-Norman Trislander in 1975. (Randak Design Consultants)

A marooned Loganair Islander gets a helping hand out of a patch of sticky sand. (H. E. Couzens)

The unusual spectacle of Loganair's Twin Otter on a snow-covered beach. (H. E. Couzens)

Departure of Loganair DHC Twin Otter G- BGPC, 15 February 1985. (Iain Hutchison)

A busy day during July 1990 for Loganair DHC-6 Twin Otters G-BGEN and G-BEJP.
(Photo: Nigel Davidson, via Mrs Mona Davidson)

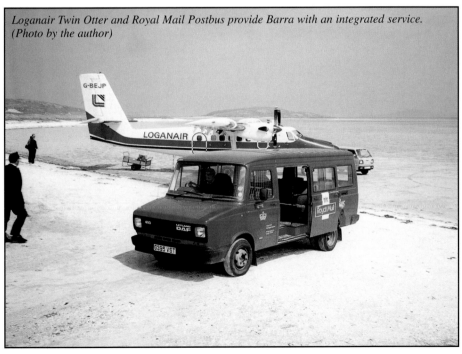

Loganair Twin Otter and Royal Mail Postbus provide Barra with an integrated service.
(Photo by the author)

Loganair Shorts 360 in Manx Airlines colours prepares to land. (Photo by the author)

Splashdown accomplished. (Photo by the author)

5

"Fresh Row over Shorts on the Beach"

The newspaper headline writers had a field day during the summer of 1994. Their interest had been attracted by the public protest which followed the introduction of a new type of aircraft on to the Barra air service. The above headline, which appeared in *The Scotsman*, was just one, and it had nothing to do with beachwear! Others included, "Latest flight cancellations fuel concerns over Barra air service" and "Crunch talks as Barra air service chaos reaches crisis point" in the *West Highland Free Press*; and "Loganair could lose its Barra franchise" in *The Scotsman*. 1994 was a year of incredible change for the air service to Barra. It hit the news all summer and unfortunately the attention was mostly of the kind which Loganair could have done without.

In 1992, the airline had intimated that the Twin Otter would, in five years or so, be coming to the end of its useful life and that it was looking to replace it, the 844th and final Twin Otter having come off the production line in 1988.

Nothing suitable, with a fixed undercarriage, was available as a replacement, but the airline already had a fleet of Shorts 360 aircraft and consultations began with the manufacturers on adapting it for the unique conditions of the Tràigh Mhòr. The Belfast-built airliner had first flown on 1 June 1981 and was an upgrading of the earlier Shorts 330, itself a development of the Shorts SC7 Skyvan.

The discussions with Shorts and the Civil Aviation Authority eventually resulted in the first test landing at Barra on 30 June 1993 when, after several aborted attempts, the first successful touchdown was made by G-BMAR at 1920 hours. The aircraft approached from the west over the road between *Suidheachan* and the airport terminal. Many more test landings had to be carried out, as adjustments were made to the aircraft by engineers, before it was decided before the end of 1993 that the passenger-carrying service could be undertaken. To achieve this, Runway 07/25 was lengthened to 1,500 metres at the Orosay end and some levelling of the beach was carried out in this area. The regulatory authority, the CAA, insisted that fire cover at the airport be increased. The authority also insisted upon the closure of the road when the aircraft was due and this led to the appearance of traffic lights between the passenger terminal and *Suidheachan*.

Introduction of the Shorts 360 had in fact been timetabled as commencing on 3 January 1994 from both Glasgow and Benbecula. While the Glasgow service continued as a Twin Otter operation for a further three months, the Shorts 360 did continue to Barra from Stornoway and Benbecula from January. With the planned introduction of the Shorts 360 on the Glasgow route now in place, the two remaining Twin Otters in the fleet, G-BMXW and G-BEJP, were quickly put up for sale. The need to increase fire cover to Category 3 led to Loganair giving up management of the airport and responsibility passed to Highlands and Islands Airports Ltd (HIAL) on 27 March. The last official Twin Otter service had arrived the previous day. Loganair's Scott Grier and HIAL's Hugh Lawson flew out to Barra on Sunday 27th but in a Twin Otter as the Shorts 360 could not be used due to 45 mph winds at Barra. They were there to greet the first scheduled Shorts 360 service from Glasgow on Monday 28th but, due to poor visibility at Barra, this only got as far as Tiree. After a lengthy wait at Tiree in the hope that conditions at Barra might improve, the aircraft had to return to Glasgow when the tide at Barra turned. The first scheduled Shorts 360 service arrival at Barra eventually took place on Tuesday 29 March. These problems were an indication of things to come.

Loganair was also undergoing radical restructuring during the first months of 1994. Airlines of Britain Holdings was endeavouring to stem losses at its Glasgow-based subsidiary and, at the end of March, all services to south of the border were transferred to sister company, Manx Airlines Europe. The Scottish airline would, in future, concentrate on core routes in the Highlands and Islands as well as those to Northern Ireland, employing both a much reduced complement of staff, and aircraft consisting of Britten-Norman Islanders and Shorts 360s. Some Shorts 360s in the Manx fleet were transferred to Loganair and, for a while, 360s with Loganair colours and titles were interspersed with those still in Manx livery but carrying Loganair titles. It made for colourful activity on the Tràigh Mhòr and there were to be further livery variations before the year was over.

Scott Grier, Loganair's Managing Director, tried to undertake a management buy-out but this failed when Airlines of Britain Holdings decided not to sell. By this time, Loganair had already announced that, as from 11 July 1994, the company would become a franchisee of British Airways and thus the Shorts 360 fleet began to appear in British Airways livery.

Criticism of the Shorts 360 on the Barra run mounted almost from the start of operations by the larger aircraft. Passenger capacity was limited to about two thirds of the aircraft maximum due to the nature of the landing strip at Barra. The introduction of the 360 also meant the combination of the Tiree and Barra services into the one schedule. This, it was was claimed, further restricted the number of seats to Barra. However it was overlooked by detractors that operations via Tiree were a normal occurrence every winter even on the Twin Otter schedule. Capacity restrictions were in fact aggravated by a regulatory decision that increased the average weight used for calculating aircraft trim for an adult male from 84kg to 92kg and this applied equally to the Shorts 360 and the Twin Otter, as indeed it did to other aircraft types operating far from the sands of Barra.

The Shorts 360's need of a longer runway than that required by the Twin Otter made its operation much less flexible. The Shorts 360 could only use the extended Runway 07/25. Increased visibility was required and the 360 was more susceptible to cross-winds. New rules had been laid down which prevented operations if standing water was greater than a certain level. This, and the reaching of the lengthened runway by the tide sooner than previously, combined to further restrict aircraft movements.

In June, it was reported to a meeting of the airport consultative committee that, of 57 flights scheduled between Glasgow and Barra between 28 March and 1 June 1994, seven had been cancelled and eight delayed. Things seemed to come to a head in July, the weekend immediately before the relaunch as British Airways Express. The aircraft was unable to land for three days in succession. On Saturday 9 July there was poor visibility, and on both Sunday 10 and Monday 11 July, there was too much standing water on the beach.

Having witnessed the difficulties caused by the aircraft's failure to land on the Tràigh Mhòr, Calum Macdonald, the Labour MP for the Western Isles, tabled a Parliamentary Question. "As the Glasgow-Barra service was the only one in Scotland to receive a Government subsidy, what steps was the Secretary of State for Scotland taking to monitor the performance of this service?" Islanders were asking how the 'plane would be able to land in December, if it could not land in July.

The *West Highland Free Press* reported on 22 July 1994 that, in the seven days up to Tuesday 19 July, three out of nine possible Glasgow flights had not arrived, nor had three out of six Stornoway services. On one occasion mail did not arrive for three days in succession and islanders travelling to or from Glasgow or Stornoway, often for healthcare, found themselves stranded. In the middle of this difficulty, Loganair and Highlands and Islands Airports Ltd staged a long-planned emergency exercise involving the simulated crash of a Shorts 360 on the beach.

A public meeting of the Eoligarry Airport Consultative Committee held in Castlebay on 25 July gave the islanders the opportunity to raise concerns about the Shorts 360. It was most unfortunate for Scott Grier that the scheduled Shorts 360 service, taking him to Barra for the meeting, was unable to land on the Tràigh Mhòr and was diverted to Tiree with the passengers later being shuttled in two groups to Barra in an Islander. One protester commented that the aircraft was well named as it flew to Barra and turned 360 degrees and went back again without landing. The meeting understood what he meant even if the arithmetic wasn't quite accurate! The meeting also heard of a Loganair plan to base an Islander at Barra to carry diverted passengers between Barra and Benbecula. The local authority had previously raised the idea of a helicopter link between the two islands. London-based Moscow Applied Scientific Services at one point told *The Scotsman* that they would organise a visit to Barra of the Irkutsk manufactured BE-200 amphibious aircraft to let islanders see how it would cope with the Tràigh Mhòr conditions. However, nothing more was heard of this proposal.

Reliability of the Shorts 360 did improve with the relaxation of some of the operating restrictions but by then the aircraft's credibility had already been seriously damaged and much emotion had been generated in the debate. When difficulties arose with the operation, it was the image of the aircraft bearing the 'Loganair' name which accompanied any problem, while there was often a failure to appreciate that bureaucracy was placing ever increasing handicaps on the carrier in its operation of a unique service, handicaps which would have applied equally to the Twin Otter operation. As a result of the high profile occupied by the airline, but less so on bureaucrats at various levels, pressure mounted on Loganair during the autumn of 1994 with *The Scotsman* reporting that the Scottish Office minister responsible for the subsidy arrangements had given Loganair an ultimatum to improve reliability or face the service going out to tender. In October, a BBC Radio crew, on the island to make a programme about the problems experienced throughout the summer with the air service, found itself stranded when, on the day they were due to fly back to Glasgow, the aircraft was unable to land.

In fairness to Loganair, it should be recorded that the airline expended a generous effort in its endeavours to maximise its fleet, provide a high standard of service to island, and accommodate the various conditions laid down by various aviation and local bodies. Faced with such an onslaught of hostility, Loganair could have given the statutory notice required to withdraw from the service and departed to concentrate its energies on other aspects of its business. It did not do this. Instead, its commitment to Barra was shown when, on 4 November 1994, the airline announced that a Twin Otter would return to the route. The airline had been able to charter one from the Norwegian carrier, Widerøe, and the familiar Twin Otter resumed service to Barra on 30 November, still wearing its Norwegian registration and colours.

During the debate on the obsolescence of the Twin Otter, it had been reported that there were still in excess of 500 of the type in service around the world and that spare parts were unlikely to be a problem in the immediate future. However, this information was of dubious validity. While there were still many Twin Otters in operation, the figure had been calculated, not from catalogued data of airworthy aircraft, but by elimination of withdrawn or written off machines, the recording of which was open to substantial fallibility. The number of Twin Otters still flying in Europe was very low, while availability of parts at reasonable cost has been variable. Indeed, efforts to obtain a back-up aircraft, once the decision had been taken to return to Twin Otter operation, revealed that scarcity had resulted in high prices being demanded for machines of substandard condition, and the quest to add a second Twin Otter had to be abandoned. Fortunately, the reliability of the sole Twin Otter has been such that it has served the island with almost unwavering regularity since its reintroduction. The events of 1994 are now in the past, yet there must surely never have been an eight months like it since the air service to Barra began in 1936. However, in the long term it may prove that continued beach operations to Barra by the Twin Otter, rather than representing a problem solved, merely represent a problem postponed. ✈

6

The Hard Runway Saga

"On Barra, you can still see Otters on the beach."
Holiday brochure, 1999.

For sixty years and more, Barra has relied upon the shoreline for its airport facilities. Northern & Scottish Airways first used the Tràigh Mhòr for scheduled services in 1936 following Captain David Barclay's lack of success in identifying a suitable location for a grass landing strip.

In 1971, the Army offered to construct a strip on the machair between Tràigh Mhòr and Tràigh Eais under its Operation Military Aid to the Community (OPMAC) scheme. The cost was then estimated at £80,000 but, while other islands such as Skye acquired airstrips under this arrangement, the Barra proposal never got off the ground because of fears about coastal erosion and damage to the dune and machair belt.

By 1993, Comhairle nan Eilean felt that a hard runway was inevitable given that the DHC-6 Twin Otter had been out of production for five years and no other suitable aircraft with a fixed undercarriage was available. It was believed that a hard runway would guarantee the future of the air service and allow greater operational flexibility. Loganair already had the Shorts 360 in its fleet and it investigated the possibility of adapting this aircraft type for operations at the Tràigh Mhòr.

On 14 April 1993, the Council commissioned a feasibility study report on the provision of a hard runway for the island from Airport Management Services Ltd, a subsidiary of Highlands and Islands Airports Ltd. By the time the preliminary report was delivered in July, Loganair and Civil Aviation Authority engineers had achieved the first successful landing of the Shorts 360 on the Tràigh Mhòr. This was on 30 June 1993 although it was not until the following year that it was introduced to scheduled services.

Airport Management Services Ltd considered seven sites, four of which were located on Barra while three were on the neighbouring island of Vatersay which is now linked to Barra by a causeway. Some of the sites were quickly eliminated from the seven suggested for consideration but the contenders were Bearnasdale, Allasdale, Tràigh Mhòr and Tràigh Scurrival on Barra. On Vatersay, they were Vatersay Bay, Heishival and Port a' Bhàta.

Opinion among the population of Barra was sharply divided as to the need for what would be an expensive project which also appeared to lack the support of the incumbent airline. The Heishival site was on a raised plateau and would have been subject to weather constraints. It was quickly rejected. Port a' Bhàta, west of the Vatersay settlement of Caolis, was also excluded because of approach obstacles. The Bearnasdale site, perhaps better described as an east/west location at Borve machair, was rejected for several reasons, one of which would have been the requirement for the runway to traverse the public road.

The Vatersay Bay and Tràigh Scurrival sites both involved land reclamation from the sea. Vatersay Bay was felt to be a high cost option, partly due to poor access, and a public road crossing the runway would have been necessary here too although, strangely, the report did not mention that. At Scurrival, which is at the very north of Barra, almost the entire runway proposed would have had to have been reclaimed from the sea.

The Allasdale site was considered possible, despite high ground offset to the west and lying north of the proposed runway. This site was considered to have the lowest cost for building a runway but, compared to Tràigh Mhòr, added cost would arise for the areas on which the apron and terminal building would have to be accommodated.

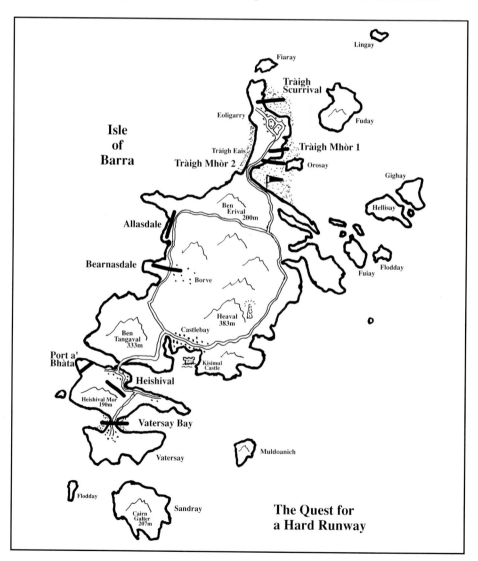

The Quest for
a Hard Runway

In the end, the report came down in favour of a location at Tràigh Mhòr and two options were offered, both of which utilised the existing terminal building. The road to Eoligarry would need to be diverted and both options had problems with the approaches due to high ground to the south and because of the area's location within Scottish Natural Heritage's designated Site of Special Scientific Interest. The Tràigh Mhòr 1 option located the runway entirely on grazing land to the north of the beach and would have required the removal of a small hill, Cnoc Chiall. The Tràigh Mhòr 2 option located the runway slightly further to the south, partly on land, partly on the beach and would have been the cheaper engineering solution, although the end of the runway would have been 250 metres from the terminal and would have needed a taxiway. Both Tràigh Mhòr options would have required some lowering of the dunes at the southern end of Tràigh Eais. Tràigh Mhòr 2 would have had less effect on grazing land and excavated rock could have been used for the foreshore infill.

Comhairle nan Eilean considered that the hard runway would permit greater flexibility as flights would no longer be dependent upon tide conditions but Loganair believed that this was open to doubt. If wind conditions change, the beach offers pilots a large expanse of tidal flats, unlike a singular hard runway. Crofters at Eoligarry had particularly strong objections to Tràigh Mhòr 1 because of the quality of the grazing which would have been threatened.

Excluding the cost of environmental assessments, public consultation and enquiry, land acquisition, etc., the cost of Tràigh Mhòr 2 was estimated, in 1993, at £4.30 million. This site was suggested as the preferred option. In 1994, Loganair introduced the Shorts 360 to service but, as narrated in the previous chapter, had to replace it once more with the Twin Otter by the end of that year. Local cocklers and environmentalists, who had been concerned about damage to the beach by the heavier Shorts 360, were also concerned about the effects of the proposed runway on coastal and marine processes. Other island interests were more concerned about the provision of a reliable air service.

One reason for considering the hard runway had been the anticipated lack of a Twin Otter in the near future but, in the short term at least, the type is now back in service at Tràigh Mhòr. Concerns had also been expressed over the years about the continuing commercial extraction of shell from the beach and its effects, but this was no longer a consideration after 1996 with the closure of Barra Shell. However, discussions were continuing between interested parties and, during the summer of 1996, Comhairle nan Eilean decided to hold a local referendum on the issue of a permanent airstrip. Some people however noted that they were being asked to vote on a proposal about which they were being provided with inadequate information.

The ballot paper contained two questions. The first question asked, "Do you want a hard landing strip to replace the beach landing strip for scheduled passenger services?" The second question was, "Do you want any hard landing strip to be at Tràigh Mhòr?" In a 61.12% turnout, 365 islanders voted in favour of the first question, with 235 rejecting the proposal for a hard runway. On the second question, 217 voted in favour of the Tràigh Mhòr site, but 280 rejected it as the proposed location.

The construction of a hard runway would have needed funding assistance from the

European Union and would have had to compete against other projects for this. These included the now completed causeway between North Uist and Berneray. There were those who felt that a Sound of Barra car ferry service and a causeway between South Uist and Eriskay should take priority over a runway for Barra's air services. The local referendum, while not binding, left Comhairle nan Eilean with a dilemma. A majority of the islanders who voted wanted a hard runway - but not at the site which had been declared most suitable.

In 1998, the Council's Barra and Vatersay Local Plan stated that, "The Council has resolved to delete the airstrip opportunity from the Adopted Plan. It will nevertheless continue to liaise with Highlands and Islands Airports Ltd and the Scottish Office to ensure protection of the Barra air service. Any proposal for a permanent airstrip in the future, whether at Tràigh Mhòr or elsewhere, would have to be judged against the Plan as Adopted or would be the subject of a formal modification to the Plan which would be advertised. In either event, the proposal would also require an Environmental Assessment."

The latest round of EU structural funding began in 1999. The less well-off regions of Europe receive support through a series of funds known as the Structural Funds, which give financial assistance to public bodies. Until now, the Highlands and Islands have qualified for Objective One funding (£242 million for 1994-1999) designed "to achieve structural adjustment and development of the less developed regions." These regions are those where Gross Domestic Product per head is less than or close to 75% of the European Union average. In Scotland, only the Highlands and Islands qualified for Objective One funding, although many other parts of Scotland also receive assistance under other schemes.

Communications featured within the main priorities for Objective One funding but revised criteria for the next European Objective One programme from January 2000 meant that the Highlands and Islands narrowly failed to qualify. However, a transitional funding package of £210 million over the next six years was negotiated by the Government and welcomed with much relief by many in the Highlands and Islands.

Under European Union rules, Comhairle nan Eilean Siar has to put the subsidised inter-island Stornoway-Benbecula-Barra air service out to tender every three years, an exercise which was repeated during the summer of 1998. This was again based on the beach operation at Barra with British Regional Airlines intimating in advance that they would not re-tender. Loganair was the only company to submit a bid and it was awarded the contract "subject to some variations in the bid and also depending on a successful approach to the Scottish Office to meet some of the extra costs involved because of the lower passenger numbers since the Sound of Harris ferry came into operation."

Many people now believe that the proposal for a hard runway at Barra is already "dead in the water". Whether this is true remains to be seen but the lack of such a facility may make it increasingly difficult to satisfy Barra's future air service needs. ✈

7

The Tràigh Mhòr today

"The sea shore is the meeting place of sea and land. It is for that reason the most fascinating and the most complex of all the environments of life." C. M. Yonge in *The Sea Shore,* 1949.

In this book we are concerned with the aviation activity on the Tràigh Mhòr, but the above quotation is a reminder of the attraction of the sea shore to the naturalist. To Donald Manford and many others, the attraction of the Tràigh Mhòr is the cockle. Manford was born and brought up on Barra and has been involved in cockling to varying degrees since childhood. Quantities have declined quite dramatically in recent years as a result of over-fishing, fishing in the breeding season and, according to Manford, destruction of the seed beds by the Shorts 360 in 1994.

The number of people involved in the fishery can vary from five to fifty, numbers fluctuating due to such factors as weather conditions and market values. Donald tells me that cockles can be located by following the outgoing tide when they are only partly submerged. They are found in the mid-tide range, generally about three hours down from high tide along the length of the beach. Where the beach is dry, they can also be detected by their breathing eye. The cockles are sold to a variety of fish traders and exported mainly to France and Spain by road transport. A few, however, go to local hotels where they are sometimes described as, "Barra cockles … from our airport.". Liaison is maintained with the airfield operator to ensure that the interests of both parties are safeguarded as much as possible.

The Tràigh Mhòr and much of the north end of Barra is owned by the Government through the Scottish Executive Rural Affairs Department, by dint of a government agency in the early years of the twentieth century buying the land to allocate 'land raiders' their own crofts. The Department leases the airstrip to Highlands and Islands Airports Ltd which owns and operates the supporting aviation infrastructure. In view of the scientific and landscape value of this part of the island, various designations aid its conservation. The beach forms a large part of the Site of Special Scientific Interest while the Eoligarry isthmus is also a Geological Conservation Review Site of National Importance. Much of the area is designated an Environmentally Sensitive Area. The north of Barra and smaller, neighbouring islands such as Fuday, Fiaray and Orosay are also of international importance for wintering and passage of Greenland barnacle geese, and of national importance for wintering ringed plover, sanderling, purple sandpiper and turnstone.

While Barra and the rest of the Outer Hebrides have a much lower rainfall than many parts of the west coast of the Scottish mainland, the speed with which smaller islands such as Gighay and Hellisay can be blotted out illustrates how weather affects all aspects of island life. Air transport is no exception. Wind is a constant feature in the Hebrides and, due to the beach location of the airport, there are a number of constraints placed upon air operations, not least of which is the twice daily ebb and flow of the tide during the lunar day of twenty-four hours and fifty minutes.

Should you ever see the Twin Otter appear out of the swirling mist and splash down in pools of water on the beach, you will be relieved to know that the unique conditions at the Tràigh Mhòr require Loganair's pilots to undertake several landings under instruction before being permitted to perform the task while in command of the aircraft. Even greater familiarity with the airport is required before a pilot is cleared to bring the air ambulance aircraft in under cover of darkness.

The casual visitor will not realise that there are actually three 'runways', the thresholds of which are marked by the striped poles which can be seen along the shoreline at either side of the terminal or far out on the beach. Runway 15/33 was the longest at 846 metres but Runway 07/25 was extended to 1,500 metres during 1994, when the Shorts 360 was in service. Runway 07/25 is currently 700 metres in length and Runway 11/29 is 667 metres. Runway 15/33 is the one which experiences the greatest use.

As a rule, aircraft do not land less than three hours either side of high water, although this is not always the case. Pilots landing after high tide may, like Linton Chilcott of Air Alba writing in the magazine *Pilot*, find themselves playing the game of "spot where the ocean ends and the runway begins" as large expanses of standing water are frequently left behind. Strong easterly winds can also hold the tide in. Restricted daylight hours in winter further limit the scheduling possibilities for Loganair. Gales can be problematic upon occasion but it is visibility which will more often dictate whether, or not, a flight will land. Occasionally passengers from Glasgow find themselves back there within a couple of hours of leaving, never having seen the Isle of Barra, while the waiting passengers at Barra will have heard, but not seen, the aircraft circling. Cross winds of more than 25 knots in dry conditions (less in wet) will prevent the aircraft taxying, while higher than usual tides can mean delays to the arrival of a flight.

Airfield weather data is provided to Loganair by the HIAL staff who also send a tidal report to Loganair's operations department at Glasgow each day prior to departure of the outbound flight. Loganair staff at Barra continue to act as auxiliary weather observers for the Met Office, the data being reported by computer link. Barra is seldom under snow, although this did occur at Christmas 1995 and, even if the tide is out when a snowfall occurs, snow will generally not lie much below the high water mark due to the salty and wet conditions on the beach.

Small streams at the south end of the landing area have caused problems over the years. One was lined with sandbags to keep it away from the landing strip after it was decided that it was the stream which was compromising the future use of the beach as an airstrip and not Barra Shell removing its raw material.

As some pilots have discovered over the years, the Tràigh Mhòr is not the place to become bogged down. Pilots have to beware of wheel sinkage which could be particularly embarrassing during an incoming tide. Occasionally, an aircraft has required a bit of motorised assistance to get it out of a sticky situation. Venture too near the low water mark and, as Linton Chilcott put it, "the *terra* may not be so *firma*". There are no repair or refuelling facilities at Barra and, should an aircraft become incapacitated, it will generally require to be hauled off the beach and beyond the high water mark.

In addition to Loganair's Twin Otter operation and the Islander's appearance on air ambulance duty, the Tràigh Mhòr sees occasional visits by privately-owned light aircraft, which have recently included a vintage de Havilland Tiger Moth, and by air taxis. Light aircraft arrivals jumped from six in 1995 to fifteen in 1996. Fourteen were recorded in 1997. Night operations do not take place at Barra except for occasional air ambulance flights when temporary arrangements have to be put in place to illuminate the strip for the arrival of the Islander. Low intensity battery lights are used with approximately twenty-two to twenty-four required, at intervals of 50m to 60m, in order to illuminate one of the two runways authorised for use at night.

If tidal conditions are normal, the flight from Glasgow will operate in the morning, and the little passenger terminal by the shore will start to come to life at about 0815 hours. The building, situated on the edge of the machair, is now almost twenty years old but has the facilities necessary for its modest level of use and was remodelled in 1997. Barra's airport may be a natural creation but it is also an expensive facility to operate. As with all the airports owned by Highland and Islands Airports Ltd, with the notable exception of Sumburgh, Barra operates at a loss (£332,000 in 1998/99) despite annual support to the Company from the Government. It is hardly surprising therefore that the Conservative Government (1992-1997), proactive in selling off state assets, realised that HIAL would not be attractive to private enterprise. However, as with so many other aspects of Highland life, the value of the airport to the island cannot be measured solely in financial terms.

First duties of the day for the fire crew include cleaning the terminal building, other accommodation, and the fire station. The flight information officer will send the latest weather information and position of the tide to Loganair Operations at Glasgow Airport. Glasgow Weather Centre is also provided with hourly weather reports during the airfield's opening hours.

The terminal's passenger waiting area, with seating for about twenty-five, has a refreshment counter run by Co-Chomunn Bharraidh, an island cooperative. During summer, Penny Mackinnon dispenses tea, coffee, light snacks and souvenirs; during the winter months, refreshments are provided by a vending machine. The waiting area overlooks the beach and one wall has a beautiful mosaic in shell, by Margaret Somerville, which illustrates local bird life. Behind the Check-in Desk are the Loganair offices and air crew rest room. Beneath the observation room of the tower is the airport manager's office, crew room, showers and toilets, an exercise room, drying room and apparatus store room. There are no long walks to aircraft at this airport so that the only piers and jetties to be found on Barra are at the island's harbours! Other airport paraphernalia, such as television monitors, drop-flap indicators and public address announcements, are also absent. There is no high security fence but public safety remains paramount. Notices at the terminal and around the beach warn people to keep off the landing area when the windsock is flying.

Around 0845 hours, a Flight Information Systems Officer (FISO) will begin a beach inspection. This has to be undertaken each day before the flight arrives in order to ensure that the last tide has not left debris on the beach which might cause damage to the aircraft or cause an accident. There are no sheep on Eoligarry land but, until fencing was improved, Eoligarry cattle occasionally wandered on to the beach. One guidebook noted that "you can tell something is going to happen when the fire engine sets out to chase the cows away, the driver slapping his door and shouting bovine insults in Gaelic."

At 0930 hours the windsock is raised to indicate the official opening of the airport. Cocklers, holidaymakers and others not involved in airport operations should now stay off the airfield. There is no air traffic control at Barra to assist pilots and operations are strictly on visual rules. The low level of air traffic means that the airfield can work on the Aerodrome Flight Information System (AFIS). After HIAL took over operations in 1994, an AFIS watchroom was established at the south end of the terminal building in temporary accommodation perched on a freight container. In 1997, this was replaced by the tower with its observation deck, creating a new landmark for the beach. *Barra Information* provides approaching and departing aircraft with just that - information and advice over the radio, but not 'control' as at busier airports. Some of the fire crew, including Hugh Douglas and Michael Galbraith, are trained as Flight Information Systems Officers – but principally it will be administration officer, Jeannie Grant, who undertakes this task. The new tower has not altered their jobs but has considerably improved the Flight Information Systems Officer's view over the Tràigh Mhòr, especially to the north-east where previously there was a blank spot. Various landmarks enable the level of visibility to be quickly calculated for relay to the approaching pilot. One of the few reminders of the past to be seen at the airport is a large scale map, framed behind the Loganair check-in desk. On this, numerous landmarks are indicated with their distance from the airport. High ground around Tràigh Mhòr, such as Ben Eoligarry (102m), Ben Erival (200m) or Ben Stack (122m), the highest point on Eriskay, is used to assess cloud height. Other landmarks, such as Crannag and the island of Orosay (both 1,000m distant), the islet of Greanamul (4,000m), a cottage at the south end of Tràigh Cille-bharra (1,500m), and Hellisay (5,500m) enable the range of visibility to be established. The weather minima for approach is 550 feet and 3km of visibility. It is a credit to Loganair that, even in winter, operations have a good record of reliability, and cancellations, for whatever reason, are rare.

As the incoming aircraft is awaited, passengers and visitors mill around the terminal. As you would expect on an island in the heart of the Gaeltacht, much of the conversation is in Gaelic. The beach has often been romanticised as the Great Cockle Shore but the airfield was called North Bay, or sometimes Northbay, in the early timetables. In reality it is some distance from the community of that name, although in earlier days that was where the agent was located, and it is situated on land between Àrdmhòr and Eoligarry townships. North Bay/Northbay may have been chosen because it was the simplest name for non-Gaelic speakers, as would be most staff and crew at Renfrew and most passengers from the mainland. When the first road signs appeared, these indicated *Northbay Airport*. The form *North Bay* still appears as the local name for the airport in both the British Airways timetable and the OAG Overseas Airways Guide. New signs at the airport in English and Gaelic refer to *Barra Airport / Port-adhar Bharraidh*. To the airline computer, it is BRR - the three-letter International Air Transport Association code used for the purposes of inter-airline communications including reservations and baggage tracking. To the governmental International Civil Aviation Organisation, Barra is encoded EGPR and this is used in Loganair documents such as log books and flight plans.

HIAL regulations require that a minimum of four fire crew are on duty. It might be Duncan MacLean, Joe Gillies, Iain MacLean and Donald McKiggan who are rostered for 'local standby' which requires manning the appliances in a state of readiness for the arrival of the flight. Three new fire appliances have recently been delivered and two will always be in service at Barra with the third in Benbecula for servicing. These are Land Rover 6 x 6 vehicles with 3.9 litre V8 petrol engines and a water-carrying capacity of 1,000 litres.

During the tourist season, camera shutters 'click' and heads turn as the Loganair pilot brings the Twin Otter safely down on to the hard sand of the Tràigh Mhòr after the sixty-five minute flight from Glasgow. The ritual of the small aircraft landing on the beach attracts such a high level of interest from visitors that the Western Isles Tourist Board lists it in its annually produced guide alongside such traditional attractions as Kisimul Castle. It is not unusual to see tour coaches, sometimes vintage models from the 1950s and 60s, unload passengers to view the event during an island excursion. These may form part of an extensive Hebridean holiday or may be shore visits coinciding with calls by such cruise vessels as the luxury *Hebridean Princess*. This interest in the unusual airport is catered for by Co-Chomunn Bharraidh as the Twin Otter, often accompanied by another beach resident, the oyster-catcher, appears on postcards, T-shirts, sweatshirts, calendars, pens, mugs, and tea-towels. Few airfields of similar size can have featured so often in photographs, television programmes, films, books, newspapers, magazines, tourist brochures and holiday videos.

Part of the enduring attraction to visitors must also be the informality of the airport, although a little of this does tend to disappear with the passing of each year. The former wooden passenger hut was replaced by the present building in 1978. Fences and gates were later erected in front of the building where before there were none. The construction work of 1997 represents a further change. The rutted machair immediately in front of the terminal has disappeared under concrete and the growing number of signs is, well, a sign of the times.

With the arrival of the aircraft, the multi-disciplined fire crew miraculously turn into baggage handlers for fifteen minutes, before reverting to firefighters just before the aircraft leaves for Benbecula. During the hour and ten minutes before the Twin Otter arrives back at Barra, the firefighters are occupied with routine duties such as checking fire extinguishers, hydrants and breathing apparatus as well as airport maintenance. An official rest break is also scheduled - there are cockles at the 'front door' and a former chef amongst the crew!

With the return of the scheduled service from Benbecula and its onward dispatch to

Glasgow, the airport then officially closes and the windsock is lowered. The firefighters have to make sure that all equipment is correctly cleaned and stored. This is followed by fire service training, a legal requirement of at least one hour having to be performed daily. The fire crew go off duty at 1345 hours but the airport manager and one leading firefighter continue with administration and other airport duties until 1615 hours.

Outwith these hours, the staff are required to turn out should an ambulance flight be expected. Barra's airport firefighters are trained to the same high standard as firefighters at other airports and they have all attended a minimum of six weeks at the Fire Training School at Teesside Airport. The work of the firefighters at Tràigh Mhòr is certainly varied as they are also involved in painting, bird control, first aid, vehicle repairs, meteorological observation, FISO duties, cleaning, testing fire alarms, and health and safety requirements. Unlike firefighters at other airports, they occasionally find themselves forking seaweed from runways and trying to move sand banks. ✈

1996 airfield personnel. Left to right: Duncan MacLean, Hugh Douglas, Maggie Campbell, Michael Galbraith and Keith Rendall. (H. E. Couzens)

8

Passage to Barra

"The sudden tumble from the skies over the Isle of Barra towards the beach of Tràigh Mhòr was a thrill included in the price of the ticket." Christopher Somerville in *The Other British Isles*, 1990.

The sea route to the isles is the traditional means of exploring the Hebrides - some might say that the sea route is the only way to travel to an island. Long before flights to the islands began, Glasgow's river, the Clyde, was the highway to the isles. During the 1930s there were still 'all the way' sailings to the Hebrides from Glasgow via the Mull of Kintyre, although time could be saved by boarding at Oban. MacBraynes had for long competed with John McCallum's *Hebrides* and Martin Orme's *Dunara Castle* and tourists were offered complex itineraries which incorporated calls at island piers up and down the western seaboard.

In the years since World War Two, sea traffic to Barra has been concentrated on the Oban route. The 1930 vessel, *Lochearn*, was succeeded in 1955 by *Claymore*. Lift on/lift off car ferry facilities arrived in 1974 with *Iona* and *Claymore*, which was built in 1977. Full roll on/roll off services to Barra had to await the arrival of the sonorously named *Lord of the Isles* in 1989, itself recently relegated to Mallaig routes with the arrival of *Clansman* in July 1998.

The earliest domestic air services to thrive were those which crossed water. Air travel then came into its own and dramatically reduced journey times. However, speed comes at a price. Fares on the air service to Barra have increased somewhat since 1936 when the hurl in the Spartan Cruiser from Renfrew could be purchased for £4 single. By the summer of 1975, the single fare was £15.90, but since then the increases have been relentless and in summer 1999 the single fare from Glasgow was £94.00.

In 1936, bookings for the air service to Barra could be made at travel agents (very much thinner on the ground than they are now) or at the Northern & Scottish Airways sales office at 153 Hope Street, Glasgow. The booking cards of yesteryear have been replaced by the British Airways computerised system on which reservations for all Loganair flights are now processed. Travel agents have direct access to the British Airways reservations system via worldwide computer networks. Alternatively, passengers can call British Airways direct on its 24-hour Lo-Call telephone number which is advertised across the UK. Depending on the number of calls coming in at any one time, telephone enquiries may be answered by any one of the five Call Centres in Glasgow, Belfast, London, Manchester or Newcastle. These are not manned 24 hours-a-day so passengers calling late at night may find themselves speaking to a British Airways agent in New York - to make a reservation from Barra to Benbecula!

Details of the British Airways flights operated by Loganair Ltd are listed in the British Airways World Timetable, an alphabetical production which lists Barra between

Barcelona and Basel; and in the British Airways Scotland timetable. Summer and winter editions appear in April and November respectively. Timetable users unfamiliar with Barra must be intrigued by the reference to "Times subject to Tides". Barra's idiosyncratic airport occasionally comes as a surprise even to British Airways' call centre staff. One former resident of north Barra, having occasion to reconfirm travel arrangements for an elderly relative, remembers the surprise of the British Airways agent when informed by the caller that the flight would be unlikely to land at the time she had quoted because it coincided with the high tide.

The cost of transport to and within the islands is of constant concern not only to islanders but to agencies responsible for employment, economic development and tourism. Just as the essential shipping services require an annual subvention to the operator, state-owned Caledonian MacBrayne Ltd, air services to smaller islands such as Tiree and Barra require financial support. In the case of the Glasgow-Barra service, this comes directly from the Scottish Executive, while Comhairle nan Eilean Siar is responsible for the inter-island service linking Stornoway, Benbecula and Barra. An indication of the Council's concern about the cost of air travel is seen in its participation at the first International Conference on Air Transport in Island Territories of Europe which was held during the spring of 1998.

While air fares may seem costly, Loganair does offer a variety of fares for different segments of the market. An excursion return is available for those able to include a Saturday night in their stay and special tariffs are available to students, senior citizens, and Barrachs working away from home. Tourists from beyond Scotland can purchase British Airways' Highland Rover air ticket and include a visit to Barra in their itinerary. The visitor to the island who wishes to sample the Tràigh Mhòr experience with a quick flip to Benbecula, followed by an immediate return, was able to do so in 1999 for a comparatively modest £39.70.

Whereas passengers on most UK domestic and international departures have to pay the UK Government Air Passenger Duty, passengers to and from Barra are exempted due the small size of the aircraft used. This concession was hurriedly announced by the Government, following storms of protest from the communities of small islands dependent on lifeline air services, when the tax was introduced in the budget of autumn 1993. No doubt the concession is even more appreciated now that the Air Passenger Duty has since doubled.

Twin Otter G-BVVK usually operates the 145-mile, sixty-five minute, Glasgow-Barra service once-a-day, six-days-a-week, although an additional rotation is often scheduled on peak summer Saturdays, and upon occasion Sunday flights have also returned to the schedule. Barra was the first island in Scotland to have a post-war Sunday air service when BEA first offered one in 1968. During the winter, some flights may also call at Tiree en route to Barra, extending the journey time by about fifteen minutes.

Because Loganair's Twin Otter aircraft operates regular flights to Tiree and to Campbeltown, Barra's tidal airfield can also affect schedules on these services. Following the resumption of Twin Otter operations in November 1994, a typical day's flying for 'Victor Kilo' might have been a breakfast time round trip from Glasgow to

Campbeltown, followed by the Glasgow-Barra-Benbecula-Barra-Glasgow trip ending in the early afternoon. Next came a Glasgow-Tiree rotation, then finally a second departure for Campbeltown.

Although G-BVVK is in and out of Glasgow Airport several times daily, it is probably given little attention by travellers hurrying for Shuttle flights to London or sun charters to the Mediterranean. The small aircraft is currently turned out in the smart pearl grey and rich midnight blue livery which British Airways launched in 1985 but which is now being superseded by a new look incorporating images from cultures and communities around the world. To satisfy legal requirements as to the specific identity of the operator, *Operated by Loganair* appears on the nose of the aircraft, along with the once familiar Loganair logo.

An open bulkhead separates the flight-deck from the passenger cabin. This flight-deck access point gives passengers a unique view of activity at the 'sharp end'. The First Officer will welcome passengers on board before indicating the emergency exits and requesting that passengers read the safety cards which are contained in the seat pockets along with inflight magazines - and motion sickness bags!

Pre-flight checks completed, and permission having been received for departure, 'Victor Kilo' needs little of Glasgow's 2,658 metre runway in order to become airborne. Erskine Bridge, traversing the River Clyde, is an early landmark as the passenger sits back and begins to enjoy the unobstructed views. This is something of an advantage on the Glasgow-Barra service given the scenic nature of most of the route over the islands. It is almost tempting to lean forward and ask the pilot to go down for a closer look at certain landmarks.

Passengers unused to the Twin Otter find themselves in a compact cabin with individual seating in a 2 + 1 formation across the aisle. The aircraft is considered to have greater passenger appeal than its predecessor, the Britten-Norman Trislander where seats could only be accessed via exterior doors. Baggage, mail and newspapers will have been stowed in the holds in both the nose and the tail of the aircraft. Due to the need to accommodate a space and weight allowance for mail and newspapers, outward flights from Glasgow usually have fewer seats available for passengers than the 18 permitted on the inbound service. If demand is high however, it is not unknown for the newspapers to be left behind in Glasgow, much to the chagrin of the population of Barra. Rush hour in Castlebay's shops coincides with the arrival of the newspapers from the 'plane.

The aircraft will soon be passing over Port Glasgow, Greenock and the "Tail o' the Bank" anchorage on the Clyde where trans-Atlantic liners once moored. These are quickly followed by the sea lochs and mountains of Argyll.

The Twin Otter, previously used in large numbers by Loganair, has become very popular with Barra residents since the type was first used on the service in 1981. This is understandable given the excellent service which the Twin Otter has provided, although you might think that the aircraft has little passenger appeal. Due to its small size, there are no cabin staff, no on-board catering and no toilet on board while the noise of the two Pratt and Whitney engines, which allow a cruising speed of about 200 mph, can be intrusive. During the flight from Glasgow, 'Victor Kilo' consumes fuel at a rate of

▲ *Aircraft have right of way. (Photo by the author)*
▼ *The Twin Otter is given a wash down at Glasgow to remove corrosive salt.*
(Iain Hutchison)

▲ *Passengers board G-BVVK in time honoured fashion. (Photo by the author)*
▼ *The cabin of the Twin Otter is utilitarian but the aircraft remains popular with travellers. (Photo by the author)*

First trial landing of the Shorts 360, 30 June 1993. (H. E. Couzens)

High tide at Barra. (Photo by the author)

Final approach to the terminal by Shorts 360, G-LEGS. (Photo by the author)

approximately 10 lbs per minute, or 600 lbs per hour.

If weather conditions permit, the journey to Barra will be under visual flight rules at a height of less than 2,000 feet and will follow an almost direct track to Barra. The Gulf of Corrievreckan, Scarba, Mull, Iona, Staffa and Fingal's Cave, the Treshnish Isles, Coll and Tiree all lie beneath or near the usual route of the flight making it little wonder that Pete Irvine, in his guide, *Scotland the Best,* lists the flight to Barra as one of his ten best journeys in Scotland. During the 1970s, Loganair also flew scheduled services to Mull and Coll but nowadays the airline's operations there are limited primarily to air ambulance flights.

On days when visibility is more limited, the pilot will fly by instruments, gradually taking the non-pressurised aircraft up to the flight level given by the Scottish Air Traffic Control Centre. This may be FL85, or 8,500 feet, following the airway known prosaically as N5730 which crosses the Firth of Lorn and the Ross of Mull while all the time homing in on the VOR beacon located on Tiree. The radio station on Tiree has the important job of tracking the considerable trans-Atlantic traffic flying over the Hebrides. The aircraft descends as it approaches Tiree, approximately 100 miles from Glasgow, where the pilot alters course to a bearing of 355 degrees for the approach to Barra and locks on to the island's navigation beacon.

From Tiree, the flight continues over the open sea with little for the passenger to observe until Barra is reached. The pilot will soon be calling up the Barra tower on the radio where Jeannie Grant or one of her colleagues will be ready to provide the information about weather conditions at Tràigh Mhòr - wind speed and direction, visibility, cloud cover, temperature and barometric pressure.

For the Twin Otter pilots, such as Alex Holmes and Don Sturrock, and the islanders, the flight to Barra is routine but, for some of the passengers, the descent on to Tràigh Mhòr will be a new experience and one which will linger. Those seated on the port side of the aircraft will have views of the hills of Barra rising up from the east coast of the island and an occasional fishing boat.

The aircraft may, at this stage, be heading directly for Eriskay where a landmark at the south end of the island is used as a navigation point before undertaking final approach to Barra. Approach diagrams for use by the pilots refer to Weaver's Castle, located on Eilean Leathan, largest of the Stack Islands just off the southern end of Eriskay. Here a turn is made to port and from 500 feet the descent for the final approach to the runway begins. The aircraft is losing height at a constant rate and still the sea is beneath us. Then the water begins to give way to the expanse of sand. One regular passenger on the route told a reporter from *The Scotsman* (18 February 1994) that, "You fly in low, frequently over people out collecting cockles. It looks like you're landing on corrugated paper, because of the action of the retreating tide on the sand. When you actually go in to it, there's water flying everywhere and there's a rumble quite unlike any other kind of landing."

Under different climatic conditions, alternative approaches to the Tràigh Mhòr may be employed. This might mean over-flying the north end of Barra and then approaching the airfield from the west over Tràigh Eais and the sand dunes on to Runway 11/29. As the aircraft taxies over the hard-packed sand towards the small terminal on the shoreline, the First Officer welcomes the passengers to Barra. Those passengers who are new to Tràigh Mhòr have time to catch their breath before the aircraft comes to a standstill. The engines stop and the First Officer lowers the aircraft's internal steps.

The airport's baggage handlers descend on the aircraft to empty the two holds of passenger luggage, mail and newspapers, as the passengers disembark on to the moist sand. Outside the terminal, the red Royal Mail Postbus is in attendance, as has been its routine for more than twenty-five years, awaiting its cargo of mail bags and any passenger requiring transport to Castlebay Post Office. The postbus forms part of an integrated transport network which is detailed in a monthly timetable of services published by Comhairle nan Eilean Siar. Postbus schedules have to change with flight times which vary because of the dependence on the tides. The timetable also indicates the mainland ferry schedule and a passenger-only service across the Sound of Barra which is also governed by the tide. As bus schedules have also to coordinate with this service while simultaneously accommodating school requirements, Barra timetables require careful scrutiny.

Passengers may have an opportunity to chat with the flight crew immediately before disembarkation. On one occasion, Captain David Dyer found himself talking to a passenger who was expressing an interest in Vatersay and wishing to know if there was any aircraft wreckage to be seen on the island. As the conversation continued, it transpired that he was a survivor from a RAF Consolidated Catalina flying boat which crashed there, with three fatalities, during a night navigation exercise on 12 May 1944.

The air crew enjoy a short break at Barra but there is a schedule to adhere to and a new complement of passengers awaiting onward transport to Benbecula. This short flight is an excellent introduction to the Western Isles. As the pilot lifts the aircraft from Tràigh Mhòr, there is a good view of the islet-studded Sound of Barra where the *Du Teillay* passed before dropping anchor off Eriskay on 23 July 1745 and setting down Prince Charles Edward Stewart on Scottish soil for the first time. The South Uist coastline may be crossed close to Pollachar, once the landing place for journeys across the Sound to Eriskay and Barra but now replaced by Ludag to the east. The pilot maintains a track up the middle of South Uist, beaches and machair visible from the port window and the long chain of mountains down the eastern coastline to starboard. The northern end of South Uist is characterised by extensive lochs. Beyond are the shallows of the South Ford which separates South Uist from Benbecula. The two islands were first linked by road in 1943.

Balivanich Airport is adjacent to the much expanded community of that name which accommodates the headquarters of the South Uist rocket range and which is operated by the Defence Evaluation and Research Agency (DERA) of the Ministry of Defence. Benbecula, with its fixed surface links to both North and South Uist, is rapidly becoming the service centre for all three islands, has a large school and is soon to have its own hospital. At Balivanich, passengers from Barra to Stornoway transfer to the larger Shorts 360 for the thirty-five minute onward flight. Stornoway, the administrative centre of the Western Isles, is a further transit point for those continuing to Inverness.

Following another short turn-round, 'Victor Kilo' will be back at Barra some seventy minutes after its earlier departure. Baggage and mail will soon be loaded for Glasgow while the passengers for the mainland will be led out to the aircraft by the Station Manager or the Customer Services Agent. Once the doors have been secured, one of the fire crew takes up position in front of the aircraft while the engines are started and assures the pilot that everybody is clear of the aircraft. The aircraft takes off from the beach and Barra is once more left behind.

On one occasion I was treated to an unusual route for the inbound journey to Glasgow. To the south of Vatersay, the southern isles culminate in a number of now uninhabited islands, Sandray, Pabbay, Mingulay and, the location of Barra Head, Berneray. It was indeed very special to see Mingulay's western cliffs from such a vantage point. Days before, I had stood on the edge of the dizzying heights of the gannet covered, 229 metre, Biulacraig. I felt much more secure in the hands of the Loganair pilot as these southernmost islets, cliffs and rocks passed beneath the cabin window and he banked the aircraft to port off Barra Head lighthouse, setting course for Glasgow.

Within the hour the 'plane is descending towards Glasgow Airport over Clydebank, the birthplace of the great Cunard liners. The passengers venture into the crowded terminal while the Twin Otter awaits a little tender, loving care from ground staff to remove traces of the salty and sandy environment of Tràigh Mhòr. The flight has many advantages over the ferry but I am always left wondering, "Was it really only an hour ago that I was on a Hebridean beach?" ✈

The Twin Otter has now served Barra longer than any other aircraft type. (Photo by the author)

9

Hebridean Herons

by

Fred Barnes

D uring the sixties I well remember collecting airline timetables and I was intrigued by the remark in the BEA timetable alongside the Glasgow-Barra-Glasgow route which read, "Alteration subject to weather and tide conditions at Barra". I later discovered that the BEA de Havilland Heron aircraft landed on the beach at Barra, and hence the unusual note in the timetable. "One day," I thought, "I would fly to Barra," but, sadly, time passed by and the opportunity to fly in the Heron was missed. In June 1993, I finally flew to Barra aboard a Loganair Twin Otter to experience the beach landing. My thoughts of the Heron lay dormant until, one morning at crew briefing, when I had a conversation with Captain Vivian Gunton who had flown the type for BEA. Captain Gunton recalled his days in Scotland and said that he still had some old photographs that might be of interest. Until 1996, Captain Gunton flew an aircraft capable of flying from London to New York in under four hours, but definitely not capable of landing on the beach at Barra - whatever the tide conditions!

BEA orders a pair of Herons

In the early fifties, British European Airways (BEA) operated an extensive network of services within the Scottish mainland and to the Outer Hebrides, Orkney and Shetland Islands, flown mainly by de Havilland Rapide and DC-3 aircraft. By 30 September 1952, the Rapides, known in BEA as the *Islander* class, had been withdrawn from all routes in Scotland with the exception of the services to Barra where the aircraft landed on the beach at North Bay. BEA had decided to replace the Rapide with a modern aircraft, but that type had to be capable of both landing on the beach at Barra and undertaking air ambulance flights. In 1951 the airline had flown the prototype de Havilland Heron 1 G-ALZL on trials between 4 August and 2 September, mainly undertaking services to the Channel Islands from Northolt and Southampton. The aircraft was painted in full BEA livery for the trial and, after evaluation, BEA decided to purchase two series 1B aircraft with a higher maximum all-up weight for delivery early in 1955 for services in Scotland. The first aircraft delivered was G-ANXB on 12 February 1955, followed by G-ANXA on 23 February. Both aircraft were named after Scottish medical pioneers during a ceremony at Glasgow's Renfrew Airport on 18 March 1955. G-ANXA was named *John Hunter* and G-ANXB, *Sir James Young Simpson*. In BEA service the Herons were known as the *Hebrides* class.

During crew training prior to the start of scheduled services, the first air ambulance operation was flown on 4 March by G-ANXB. Scheduled flights began on 18 April 1955. One aircraft was allocated to the scheduled programme, while the other was used on stand-by for air ambulance work. In order to expand scheduled services and provide cover for the air ambulance commitment, a third Heron 1B was ordered, and G-AOFY was delivered on 13 April 1956 and named *Sir Charles Bell*.

BEA had also ordered a pair of new Heron 2 aircraft with retracting undercarriage in 1955 for use on the Channel Islands routes. In March 1956, BEA agreed to a route swap with Jersey Airlines and, as part of that arrangement, Jersey Airlines accepted delivery of the two Heron aircraft, G-AORG and G-AORH, intended for BEA.

Air Ambulance tragedy

On 28 September 1957, Heron G-AOFY crashed on approach to Port Ellen Airport, Islay, killing the pilot, the radio officer and the duty nurse, Sister Jean Kennedy. The aircraft had been called out on an air ambulance flight from Glasgow in appalling weather conditions to collect a seriously ill woman. This tragic loss was a blow to the Heron operation and G-AOFY was never replaced. G-ANXA was subsequently renamed *Sister Jean Kennedy* in March 1960 in memory of the nurse killed at Islay. BEA's Heron programme was revised after the loss of G-AOFY and only the Glasgow-Tiree-Barra route was flown under normal circumstances.

During the winter months, one aircraft was on planned maintenance on rotation and on some occasions a scheduled service had to be retimed or cancelled to provide an aircraft for an air ambulance contract. When BEA adopted a new livery in 1959, both Heron aircraft were repainted in the BEA 'red square' colours. Crew establishment was normally a total of six captains and five first officers, and the aircraft could accommodate up to 14 passengers.

On 30 April 1965, Captain David Barclay, who was BEA's senior Heron captain, retired after a career spanning some thirty years flying in Scotland. Captain Barclay was a father figure of the Scottish Air Ambulance Service and had flown some 1,271 of the 5,500 ambulance flights recorded at that time. For his last trip a rare event took place when Captain Barclay's daughter, a BEA stewardess, rostered on the flight with her father. The Heron did not normally carry cabin crew, but this must have seemed like an ideal moment to make an exception. Captain Barclay flew Barra-Tiree-Glasgow, and official presentations were made at each station in recognition of his sterling service to aviation in Scotland and to the Scottish Air Ambulance Service.

From 2 May 1966, all BEA services from Glasgow were transferred from Renfrew to the new airport at Abbotsinch. The Heron programme remained unchanged until the summer of 1968 when daily direct flights were introduced from Glasgow to Barra during the peak season. That was a significant change as Barra became the first Scottish island to receive scheduled services on Sundays.

The Scottish Air Ambulance Service

The Scottish Air Ambulance Service was started to enable critically ill patients to be flown to mainland hospitals from the remote islands where such facilities did not exist and alternative journeys by surface transport could be life threatening. Many flights were literally life or death missions for patients suffering from serious illness or having been injured in some form of accident. BEA started air ambulance flights after its formation in February 1947, and in April 1948 the BEA Ambulance Unit was formally set up in Glasgow, with Captain David Barclay in charge, using two Dragon Rapide aircraft and a total of three pilots and three radio officers. A duty nurse was available from the Glasgow Southern General Hospital to accompany the crew on the flight. All of the nurses were volunteers who received special training for their "flying" role. As with all emergency services, the Ambulance Unit was on standby 24 hours a day, every day, and frequently the emergency calls came at night or in the most atrocious weather conditions.

When the Heron was introduced, it was a great improvement over the Rapide, offering more room and a faster cruising speed. In ambulance configuration the Heron carried two stretchers and some medical equipment with a crew of two pilots and a duty nurse. The Ambulance Unit covered the whole of Scotland and was under contract to the Scottish Health Service which paid BEA an annual fee.

BEA's Operations Officer at Glasgow was responsible for coordinating ambulance flights once a call had been received from the local doctor. Outside normal hours, the local BEA representative had to be contacted to organise the opening of the airfield and to arrange for the patient to be taken to the airfield at the correct time. For night landings, goose-neck flares or even car headlights were used to provide a flare-path to guide the aircraft for landing at airfields not equipped with modern navigation aids such as VOR/DME or ILS. Local islanders would turn out to offer all assistance possible to the air ambulance crews irrespective of weather conditions or time of day or night. The special needs and condition of the patient often dictated which hospital was chosen for the return flight, i.e. Glasgow for the Western Isles, Inverness for the Isle of Lewis and Orkney Islands, and Aberdeen for the Shetland Isles.

On average, some 250 ambulance flights were operated annually. For the 1962/63 financial year, the BEA Report shows 350 patients carried on 283 flights, and on 23 September 1963, the 5,000th air ambulance flight was operated. BEA Herons sometimes operated to airfields not on the company's network for ambulance flights. On rare occasions when a Heron was not available, a DC-3, Dart Herald, or even a Viscount, could be used to undertake an ambulance flight provided the airfield was suitable for the type. Many islanders owe their lives to the bravery of the BEA crews and volunteer nurses.

Operations to Barra

In 1936, Captain David Barclay was touring the Western Isles reviewing suitable landing sites on behalf of Northern & Scottish Airways for proposed scheduled services from Glasgow. On the Isle of Barra no suitable landing site existed and construction of an airfield would simply not have been economic. The locals were keen to have an air service, and over dinner one evening Captain Barclay was asked if the aeroplane could land on a beach. He replied that it might be possible and the next day he was taken to

North Bay when the tide was out where the cockle-strand beach did indeed offer a possible landing site. After successful trials, services did eventually start using Dragon Rapide aircraft. Northern & Scottish Airways was later joined with Highland Airways to form Scottish Airways which was absorbed into BEA following nationalisation in 1947.

BEA replaced the Rapide with the Heron 1B as this version had a fixed undercarriage, essential for beach landings at Barra. The sand at Barra is firm enough to support the weight of an aircraft the size of the Heron and, in modern day parlance, "braking action" could be described as good. One problem is that there can be ridges in the sand in the outer bay in areas of deeper water at high tide and some shallow pools of sea water can remain at low tide. Captain Gunton recalled the common phrase, "If you can see the seagulls' legs, it is safe to land" or, in other words, there are no pools of deep water. During the winter months especially associated with south-easterly winds and low pressure, on-shore winds make the beach slow to drain.

Captain Gunton recalled a day when the Heron became unserviceable at Barra and he had to taxy the aircraft off the beach, up and over the low sand dune into the space which acted as a car park near the hut. The aircraft remained there overnight and was safe from the incoming tide. Next day the other Heron flew out to Barra with an engineer and spares to repair the stranded aeroplane. On another occasion a tractor was needed to haul the aircraft, which had stuck in the sand, off the beach after the rescue vehicle had itself become stuck trying to move the stranded aircraft. Sadly the rescue vehicle could not be freed in time and was swamped by the incoming tide, but luckily the aircraft was saved. After each service to Barra, the Herons were thoroughly washed down to prevent salt water corrosion. The main reason for the heavy winter maintenance programme for each aircraft, considering their low utilisation, was to prevent corrosion.

The End of an Era

In October 1971, both Heron aircraft were transferred to the new Scottish Airways Division of BEA and were subsequently painted in the new and final BEA livery. The Scottish Airways Division had been set up in an effort to improve financial results, but the Heron operation was never profitable and was primarily a 'social service'. In the new economic climate, costs had to be reviewed and a new aircraft type was needed to replace the aging Herons. After evaluation, the Britten-Norman Trislander was chosen as the Heron replacement and an order for three of the type was planned. However, Britten-Norman was in financial difficulties at the time and eventually a pair of Shorts Skyliners, an improved passenger version of the Skyvan, was ordered. BEA intended to use the Skyliners on routes from Glasgow to Aberdeen, Barra, Campbeltown, Islay and Tiree offering a more comfortable aircraft and, with higher utilisation, a more economic operation. One problem, though, was that the Skyliner would be too expensive to operate in the air ambulance role and, consequently, the sad decision was taken to terminate the contract with the Scottish Health Service when the Herons were withdrawn. On 8 March 1973, the first Skyliner, G-AZYW, was delivered, followed by the second, G-BAIT, on 20 April.

The last scheduled Heron service took place on 30 March 1973 when G-ANXB operated BE8747 Barra-Tiree-Glasgow. Heron aircraft then operated scheduled services on an ad-hoc basis during April as substitutes for the Skyliners, while the Scottish Air Ambulance Service contract was taken over by Loganair on 1 April 1973.

During the summer of 1973, both Herons underwent overhaul and were placed in store at Glasgow. In September 1973, G-ANXA was leased to Sierra Leone Airways to replace its damaged aircraft, 9L-LAD. G-ANXA was ferried from Glasgow to Gatwick on 26 September 1973 and the aircraft later returned to the UK and was flown to Norwich after the lease. BEA records show that G-ANXA was disposed of on 20 November 1973 and was later sold to Peters Aviation at Norwich on 9 April 1974. G-ANXB was sold to Peters Aviation on 25 October 1973. 'XA' s days ended in New Zealand where the aircraft was destroyed by fire at the hands of vandals in 1981 while 'XB is preserved in BEA Scottish Airways livery at Newark Air Museum.

The BEA Heron 1B fleet flew for some 18 years for the airline and the aircraft were seldom ever seen outside Scotland. BEA's Heron operation will always be remembered for the Scottish Air Ambulance Service and the famous beach landings at Barra.

Hebridean Herons is adapted from an article by Fred Barnes which first appeared in Issue No. 58 of the magazine Propliner in Spring 1994 and is reproduced here with the kind permission of the author. ✈

Heron G-ANXB, fire tender and air terminal in 1964. (Dr Olive Galbraith)

Elev	Var	A/D	N57 01.6		**BARRA**
0	**9°W**	REF PT.	**W007 26.2**		**AERODROME**

A/G Loganair Barra	AFIS	**D1**	
130.65	**118.075**		**13 JUN 96**

EGPR

DIAGRAM OF MARKERS A, B & C

HEADING
101 B
RED
STRIP IDENT
BLACK
WHITE

The diagram shown represents the marker as seen on approach on the reverse side the R/W heading is replaced by a black diamond.

Terminal

35

100m Starter Extension

Tidal Flats

1500 x 60m Sand
667 x 46m Sand
846 x 46m Sand
100m Starter Extension

High water mark
Powerline 20ft
High water mark
Public Footpath
Tidal Flats

07/25 – 4921ft
11/29 – 2188ft
15/33 – 2776ft

R/W	VASIS	APPROACH	THR	RUNWAY	L.DIST	SLOPE
07 (061°T)	Nil	Nil	Nil	Nil	Full	Nil
25 (241°T)					Full	
11 (101°T)	Nil	Nil	Nil	Nil	Full	Nil
29 (281°T)					Full	
15 (141°T)	Nil	Nil	Nil	Nil	Full	Nil
33 (321°T)					Full	

OTHER LIGHTING: Obstruction.

RUNWAY SURFACES
Hard sand strips below high water mark delineated by marker poles at each end. (See inset diagram).

1. Do not remain stationary with engines running near water's edge due to soft sand wheel sinkage.
2. Certain weather conditions may result in build–up of sand dunes 70ft amsl around shoreline area.
3. Strong turbulence may be experienced in sector 160° – 240° due to terrain.
4. Powerlines 20ft amsl adjacent to western boundary of landing area.

© Racal Avionics *Aerad*

Rev: AFIS, runway 07/25.

Reproduced courtesy of Racal Avionics

Conclusion

"If you once set foot on Barra, guard your heart if you would not leave it there." Iain F. Anderson in *Across Hebridean Seas*, 1937.

Attracted by the beautiful seascapes and skyscapes, the north end of Barra is a favourite part of the island for this writer and for many visitors. However, we should not forget the problems encountered by those living here on the periphery of Europe. Transport is a major, and often a divisive issue, as Caledonian MacBrayne knows from many years of experience such as when it has proposed adjustments to schedules or increases to tariffs. Loganair shared this experience in 1994 when it introduced the Shorts 360 to Barra.

At the time of writing, it is British Regional Airlines which is fielding the brickbats from both passengers and Comhairle nan Eilean Siar and attracting the vitriol of the *West Highland Free Press* following a number of incidents which have upset travellers and local authority alike on other Western Isles routes.

As Loganair approaches twenty-five years of service to Barra, its management faces the continuing challenge of sustaining the lifeline service to the island. Traffic from the local community on the Glasgow route is unlikely to increase significantly in coming years although 'green tourism' could bring an increase in visitor numbers. Barra-Benbecula loads are likely to be greatly affected by the proposed Sound of Barra car ferry service.

Loganair has a contract to operate the Glasgow-Barra service until the end of March 2000, and the inter-island service until Summer 2001. If the company was able to acquire a second Twin Otter, this would allow greater flexibility and not leave the island without the Glasgow connection when technical problems very occasionally occur. However Loganair has the difficult task of balancing its obligations towards this lifeline service, which it takes very seriously, with the commercial implications that can be all too real for a small company which has to follow some degree of fiscal control in order to maintain the stability on which the service depends.

Caledonian MacBrayne is currently investigating whether 'fast ferries' will be suitable for its operating environment. Were these to be introduced to Barra, this could also have a bearing on the future of the air service.

One would need a great deal of foresight to know what changes may occur by the year 2006 when the air service should be celebrating its seventieth anniversary. With no aircraft of suitable size for the Barra services identified as having the potential to replace the Twin Otter, it may be that the time for a hard runway has come. It is now six years since Airport Management Services Ltd produced its feasibility study for Comhairle nan Eilean Siar and, one way or the other, it appears that some hard decisions will need to be reached. Choosing a site and locating funding will remain major challenges.

For the present, however, it can still be said with confidence that today's distinctive airport and air service remain worthy successors to the ideals of the pioneers of the 'thirties. ✈

Islanders and beachcombers – the Tràigh Mhòr has room for both. (David Dyer)

Appendix 1

Eoligarry Site of Special Scientific Interest

(Reproduced by kind permission of Scottish Natural Heritage / Dualchas Nadair na h-Alba)

Planning Authority: Comhairle nan Eilean
File Reference: 402
National Grid Reference: NF 700061
OS 1:50,000 Sheet No. 31
1:25,000 Sheet No. NF 60/70
Area 449.4 hectares (1110.5 acres)

Description:

The beach, dune and machair system of the isthmus at Eoligarry, bounded to the north and south by rocky hills, is notable in Scotland for its landforms. The variation in age, chemical composition and stability of the sand and soils within the system is reflected in its natural vegetation and fauna.

Biology

Coastland: The machair extends from sea level up the southern slope of Beinn Eoligarry. The high, marram-covered dunes to the west have spectacular blow-outs and dune slacks. At the southern end of the machair is a burn with a small marsh; and damp flushes occur towards the northern end of the site. The dry machair has several interesting botanical features, including a very high density of primroses *Primula vulgaris* and is rich in moss species. The dunes and machair are used for grazing, mainly by cattle; the only cultivation is in small patches at the southern end of the machair.

Birds: The site is used by feeding, nesting and overwintering birds, including several species of national importance.

Geology

Beach Complex Landforms: This extensive beach, dune and machair complex is important for the wide range and variety of aeolian processes shown within a small geographical area. The machair forms a wedge-shaped isthmus with its apex pointing south-west, and is bounded to the east and west by beaches of shell-rich sand (calcium carbonate content over 80%, Ritchie, 1971). Tràigh Mhòr on the east, is a vast, flat, sandy area of particular interest for the profusion of intertidal banks of cockle shells *Cardium edule* and for the series of large-scale intertidal ripples and sand bars whose formation may be related to local wave patterns. Wave activity has also caused undercutting and slumping of the stable machair along the eastern coastal edge, producing a 1-2 metre vertical sand cliff. On the Atlantic coast, Tràigh Eais, with a higher mineral content in its sand, is narrower and more variable in outline, and morphological studies indicate a general eastward movement of sand from here.

The main geomorphological interest is in the dune and machair landforms which are rich in examples of typical wind erosion features of Hebridean machair. The relationships between the different stages of many of these structures are clearly exposed. Deep V-shaped blow-outs occur in the southern part of the Atlantic dunes, and a deflation plain of dissected machair spreads eastwards from the dunes above the Atlantic beach.

Destruction of the main dune ridge has resulted in the redeposition of sand hills and ridges in the centre of the isthmus, some forms of which are uncommon elsewhere in Scotland.

Remarks:

Amended boundary.
A Geological Conservation Review Site of National Importance.

Date: 27 March 1990   Previous Notifications: 1964, 1983.

✈

Appendix 2

A Chronology of Barra's airport and air services

14 Jun 1933	Captain Jimmy Orrell of Midland & Scottish Air Ferries lands Dragon Moth G-ACCZ on the Tràigh Mhòr while undertaking a three-day survey of landing sites throughout the islands.
1 Jul 1934	Northern Airways founded by George Nicholson at Cramlington Airfield, Northumberland.
21 Nov 1934	Northern Airways becomes Northern & Scottish Airways after transfer of operations to Renfrew.
1 Dec 1934	Northern & Scottish Airways launches former Midland & Scottish Air Ferries route between Renfrew, Campbeltown and Islay.
1 Jan 1935	Northern & Scottish contracts with Argyll County Council to operate air ambulance charters, followed by Inverness County Council in 1936. Between them, the two councils covered all the Hebridean islands except Lewis.
May 1935	The writer, Compton Mackenzie, begins construction of his home by the Tràigh Mhòr, which he names *Suidheachan*.
14 May 1935	David Barclay joins Northern & Scottish Airways as pilot. Promoted to Chief Pilot on 1st August.
23 May 1935	Control of Northern & Scottish Airways passes to the Whitehall Securities group, owner of United Airways and Spartan Airlines. Whitehall Securities also acquires Highland Airways.
5 Dec 1935	Northern & Scottish Airways inaugurates a twice-weekly service between Renfrew and Skye (Glen Brittle). This service was extended to Askernish, South Uist in January 1936, and to Sollas, North Uist in February 1936.
5 Feb 1936	David Barclay lands on the Tràigh Mhòr for the first time. On board the aircraft is George Nicholson, Managing Director of Northern & Scottish Airways.
9 Apr 1936	Second survey flight lands at Barra.
26 May 1936	Barclay evacuates a patient at the request of a local doctor during the course of his third survey flight with a Spartan Cruiser III aircraft.
10 Jun 1936	Commencement of scheduled services to Barra calling "on demand".
7 Aug 1936	Barra Airfield is given official licensing by the Air Ministry.
Winter 1936/37	The single air fare to Barra from Glasgow is £4. A 90-day return fare is available for £7 17s 6d.
12 Aug 1937	Northern & Scottish Airways and Inverness-based Highland Airways merge into a combined operation and become Scottish

Airways. Share-holding of the new company is Whitehall Securities, whose airline interests are represented by British Airways Ltd, 50%; London Midland & Scottish Railway Company, 40%; and David MacBrayne Ltd, 10%. As the Ministry of Transport requires MacBraynes to keep separate accounting for its aviation interests, a paper company called Western Isles Airways is formed with a 50% share-holding by both MacBraynes and Scottish Airways Ltd. Western Isles routes officially operated by Western Isles Airways although undertaken by Scottish Airways.

1938-1942	Paisley Nurses Association contracted to supply nurses to accompany each air ambulance mission.
3 Sep 1939	Announcement of war results in suspension of Western Isles air services until May 1940.
27 Jul 1940	Highland Airways' pioneer, Ted Fresson, now in charge of Scottish Airways' northern section based at Inverness, makes his first landing on the Tràigh Mhòr in DH89 Dragon Rapide G-ADAJ.
1942-1993	Volunteer nurses from Glasgow's Southern General Hospital accompany air ambulance flights.
1944	David Barclay, Chief Pilot of Scottish Airways, is awarded the MBE.
1 Nov 1945	Announcement in Parliament of Labour Government's intention to introduce a White Paper proposing the operation of all air transport services by the State.
Summer 1946	Scottish Airways operates a Renfrew-Tiree-Barra-Benbecula-Stornoway route. Glasgow-Barra single fare is £4 10s 0d.
1 Aug 1946	Civil Aviation Bill receives Royal Assent and British European Airways Corporation (BEA) begins operations, initially on continental routes only. Domestic carriers continue operating under contract to BEA.
23 Oct 1946	Eric Starling, who joined Scottish Airways in January 1946, makes his first landing on the Tràigh Mhòr.
1 Feb 1947	Scottish Airways and other domestic airlines in the AAJC group are absorbed by BEA, with headquarters at Northolt Airport, London.
6 Aug 1947	De Havilland DH89 Dragon Rapide G-AGJF written off in an accident at Barra.
30 Sep 1947	George Nicholson, founder of Northern & Scottish Airways, made redundant by BEA. He died in South Africa in 1950.
31 Mar 1948	Ted Fresson, founder of Highland Airways, made redundant by BEA.
April 1948	Air Ambulance Unit established by BEA at Renfrew, headed by David Barclay.
5 July 1948	Creation of the National Health Service results in free carriage of patients by the Scottish Air Ambulance Service.

6 Dec 1951	BEA Dragon Rapide G-AGPH crash lands at Barra while on air ambulance duty. The two elderly female patients suffered from shock, cuts and bruises. One of the women dies at home a day later. The aircraft was subsequently written off.
Feb 1955	Two new Heron aircraft delivered to BEA base at Renfrew.
27 Feb 1955	Death of 'The Coddy', John MacPherson, Barra's first airline representative.
18 Mar 1955	Naming ceremony at Renfrew of the two new Herons, G-ANXA and G-ANXB.
12 April 1956	Delivery of third Heron, G-AOFY.
28 Sep 1957	Loss of Heron G-AOFY with all on board during an ambulance flight to Islay.
31 Jan 1959	A baby girl, Belle Anne Macleod, is born on board one of the Heron aircraft taking her mother from Barra to hospital in Glasgow.
1 Feb 1962	Loganair formed as a division of Duncan Logan Construction Ltd with Duncan McIntosh as Chief Pilot.
1 Sep 1963	A baby boy, Alexander Thomas Gillies, arrives on board an air ambulance flight from Barra to Glasgow.
25 Sep 1963	Ted Fresson dies in Inverness.
1964	Tràigh Mhòr first designated a Site of Special Scientific Interest.
30 Apr 1965	Captain David Barclay retires from BEA.
2 May 1966	Abbotsinch replaces Renfrew as the airport for Glasgow.
Summer 1968	BEA operating Glasgow-Barra seven days a week making Barra the first Scottish island to have a Sunday air service.
New Year 1969	Katie MacPherson, BEA's Station Superintendent at Barra is awarded the MBE.
May 1971	The Army offers to build a permanent airstrip on Barra under the Operation Military Aid to the Community (OPMAC) scheme for £80,000.
8 Oct 1971	Eric Starling celebrates the 40th anniversary of his first solo flight with a Barra roster.
1 Apr 1972	British Airways Board formed to coordinate activities common to both BEA and BOAC with a view to merger.
30 Mar 1973	BEA withdraws its two de Havilland Heron 1B aircraft.
2 Apr 1973	G-AZYW operates the first Shorts SC7 Skyliner service Glasgow-Barra.
1 Apr 1974	BEA and BOAC officially merge as British Airways. The sign on the hut at Barra reads *British Airways Scotland*.
1 Oct 1974	Loganair begins operating Glasgow-Tiree-Barra with Britten-Norman Trislanders under contract to British Airways, before taking over the service in their own right in April 1975.
1 Nov 1975	Loganair introduces a Barra-Benbecula-Stornoway service with the Britten-Norman Islander.

11 Jun 1978	Sir Michael Herries, Chairman of the Royal Bank of Scotland, opens Loganair's new passenger terminal at Barra.
1980	Having suffered a stroke, Katie MacPherson, Loganair's Station Manager at Barra, retires after three decades of service with it and its predecessors.
24 Feb 1981	Captain David Barclay dies, aged 75.
Oct 1981	Loganair introduces the DHC-6 Twin Otter to the Glasgow-Barra run with the start of the winter timetable.
1982	Duncan McIntosh is succeeded as Managing Director of Loganair by Scott Grier.
Winter 1983/84	The single fare Glasgow-Barra, £4 in 1936, is now £40.00.
March 1984	Janet MacLean becomes Loganair's Station Manager at Barra.
1 Apr 1986	Highlands and Islands Airports Ltd formed, as an agency of the Civil Aviation Authority, to operate several of the loss-making but socially necessary airports in Scotland.
1987	Loganair comes under the Airlines of Britain Holdings umbrella with the purchase by British Midland of the 25% share-holding of Scott Grier. BMA already held the other 75%.
Dec 1988	De Havilland Canada ceases production of the Twin Otter aircraft.
1990	Site of Special Scientific Interest extended.
April 1993	Airport Management Services Ltd commissioned to produce a report on a permanent airstrip for Barra. A site on the north side of Tràigh Mhòr is selected.
April 1993	The Scottish Air Ambulance contract is split, Loganair providing Islander aircraft stationed at Kirkwall and Lerwick, and Bond Helicopters basing Bölkow 105D helicopters at Prestwick and Inverness.
30 Jun 1993	G-BMAR makes the first landing of a Shorts 360 on the Tràigh Mhòr.
15 Nov 1993	Loganair re-opens an air ambulance base at Glasgow following a review of the contract by the Scottish Ambulance Service in response to popular demand.
Feb 1994	Following a restructuring by Airlines of Britain Holdings of its relationship with Manx Airlines, Scott Grier launches a management buy-out bid for Loganair. It is unsuccessful.
26 Mar 1994	"Last" Twin Otter service into Barra.
27 Mar 1994	Responsibility for Barra Airport passes from Loganair to Highlands and Islands Airports Ltd.
29 Mar 1994	First, belated, Shorts 360 air service from Glasgow touches down at Barra.
Summer 1994	One way fare Glasgow-Barra is £80.00.
11 Jul 1994	Loganair commences operations as a British Airways Express franchisee.

4 Nov 1994	Announcement that the unpopular Shorts 360 operating on the Glasgow-Barra service will be replaced by a Twin Otter, initially leased from Widerøe of Norway.
30 Nov 1994	The Twin Otter resumes services from Glasgow.
1 Apr 1995	Control of Highlands and Islands Airports Ltd passes from the Civil Aviation Authority to the Secretary of State for Scotland.
July 1995	Loganair re-awarded Barra-Benbecula-Stornoway contract for which tenders had been invited by Comhairle nan Eilean.
Summer 1996	Loganair and Manx Airlines Europe come under the umbrella of British Regional Airlines, within the Airlines of Britain Holdings group.
July 1996	Non-binding referendum held by Comhairle nan Eilean on the future of Barra's airport. Barra Shell ceases operations after forty years of activity on the Tràigh Mhòr.
27 Oct 1996	Loganair fleet consists of Britten-Norman Islander and DHC-6 Twin Otter aircraft following transfer of Shorts 360 services to British Regional Airlines.
1 Mar 1997	Loganair Ltd becomes an independent company following a management buy-out which incorporates its Islander and Twin Otter operations. Services from Barra to Glasgow and Benbecula continue as Loganair services within the British Airways Express franchise arrangement.
1997	New control tower constructed at Barra Airport and passenger terminal is remodelled.
June 1998	Barra-Benbecula-Stornoway route awarded to Loganair on a three-year contract.
Autumn 1998	Michael Galbraith assumes the position of Airport Manager at Barra, Keith Rendall taking up a new post at Kirkwall Airport.
31 March 1999	Passenger traffic at Barra airport for the preceding twelve months is 8,842.
July 1999	With the reconvening of the Scottish Parliament after a break of 292 years, responsibility for Highlands & Islands Airports Ltd is transferred to The Scottish Ministers.
Summer 1999	One way fare Glasgow-Barra is £94.00. ✈

Heron G-ANXB bearing BEA Scottish Airways titles, July 1972. (Daniel Green)

Appendix 3

de Havilland Heron G-ANXB

De Havilland Heron series 1B, G-ANXB, construction number 14048, was one of two which served Barra continuously between 1955 and 1973 in the service of British European Airways. They were joined by a third Heron 1B, G-AOFY, between June 1956 and September 1957. G-ANXB is now preserved at the Newark Air Museum, Winthorpe, Nottinghamshire; Telephone 01636 707170.

Wingspan: 71 feet, 6 inches / 21.79 m
Length: 48 feet, 6 inches / 14.78 m
Height: 15 feet 7 inches / 4.75 m
Range: 560 miles / 900 km
Maximum speed: 183 mph / 294 kph
Loaded weight: 13,000 lbs
Power plant: Four de Havilland Gipsy Queen 30 (250 hp)

1954	Built at Chester.
Oct 1954	First flight, as G-5-14.
3 Dec 1954	Registered as G-ANXB to British European Airways.
9 Feb 1955	Certificate of Airworthiness issued.
12 Feb 1955	Delivered to British European Airways
4 Mar 1955	First operational flight from its base at Renfrew as an air ambulance.
18 Mar 1955	Named *Sir James Simpson*, later *Sir James Young Simpson*, after the Bathgate born medical pioneer.
20 Mar 1955	First visit to Barra.
1968	First Sunday visits to Barra during the summer operating schedule.
1970	Occasional rosters to Campbeltown and Islay.
Sep 1971	BEA Scottish Airways Division formed.
31 Mar 1973	G-ANXB operates last roster for BEA - from Barra, via Tiree, to Glasgow.
25 Oct 1973	Delivered to Norwich.
31 Oct 1973	BEA ownership cancelled.
19 Nov 1973	To Peters Aviation Ltd, Norwich.
7 Dec 1977	To Brunstead Holdings Ltd, Norwich.
27 Nov 1979	To Pan Universal Aircraft Services (Channel Islands) Ltd - moved to Biggin Hill, Kent.
25 Mar 1980	Certificate of Airworthiness expired.
27 Oct 1981	Collected from Biggin Hill and moved to Newark Air Museum.
1992	Restored to *BEA Scottish Airways* livery at Newark Air Museum. ✈

A Scottish aviation trilogy from Iain Hutchison

Air Ambulance

Six Decades of the Scottish Air Ambulance Service.

Foreword by R.E.G. Davies, Curator of Air Transport, Smithsonian Institution

"...crammed with great human interest stories of courage and resilience, flying prowess and sheer heroism."
James Henderson, Northern Times

Prices - £19.95 hardback; £12.95 softback

The Flight of the Starling

The flying career of Scottish pioneer aviator
Captain Eric Starling FRMetS MRAeS.

Foreword by Sir Peter Masefield

"A nice book and very heavily illustrated.." Jimmie MacGregor, BBC Radio Scotland
"A super read....a story of Scotland; a story of the changes in Scotland."
Alex Dickson, Radio Clyde

Price - £9.95

The story of Loganair

Scotland's Airline - the first 25 years.

"A most readable book, well produced and one of the most useful volumes
to cross my desk for some time past." *J.D. Ferguson, Aviation News*

Price - £4.95

All titles available from:
Kea Publishing, 14 Flures Crescent, Erskine, Renfrewshire PA8 7DJ, Scotland.
Please add 10% for postage and packing; 25% for air mail outside Europe.

Bibliography

Airport Management Services Ltd, *Feasibility Study, Barra Airstrip, Final Report* (October, 1993).

Bao, Phil Lo, *An Illustrated History of British European Airways* (Browcom Group plc, Feltham, 1989).

Barnes, Fred, 'Barra Airport - where life is a beach', *Airways*, Vol 1, No 3, July/August 1994.

Boyd, J.M. & Boyd, I.L., *The Hebrides - A Natural Tapestry* (Birlinn Ltd, Edinburgh, 1996).

Cameron, Dugald, *Glasgow's Airport* (Holmes McDougall Ltd, Edinburgh, 1990).

Campbell, John L (ed.), *Tales from Barra told by the Coddy* (Birlinn Ltd, Edinburgh, 1992).

Chilcott, Linton, 'Air Alba', *Pilot*, October 1995.

Clegg, Peter V., *Sword in the Sky* (Peter V Clegg, Godalming, 1990).

Clegg, Peter V., *Wings over the Glens* (GMS Enterprises, Peterborough, 1995).

Foster, Kenneth, 'Final Return to Barra', *The Scots Magazine*, November 1997.

Hutchison, Iain, *The Story of Loganair* (Western Isles Publishing Co Ltd, Stornoway, 1987).

Hutchison, Iain, *The Flight of the Starling* (Kea Publishing, Erskine, 1992).

Hutchison, Iain, *Air Ambulance* (Kea Publishing, Erskine, 1996).

Kinnes, Sally, 'Landing in Trouble', *Scotland on Sunday*, 20 February 1994.

Mackenzie, Compton, *My Life and Times, Octave 7, 1931-1938* (Chatto & Windus, London, 1968).

May, Garry, *The Challenge of BEA* (Wolfe Publishing Ltd, London, 1971).

Murray, W.H., *The Islands of Western Scotland* (Eyre Methuen Ltd, London, 1972).

Riddoch, Lesley, 'Strand Storm', *The Scotsman*, 19 July 1996.

Sinclair, Marion (ed.), *Scottish Island Hopping* (Polygon Books, Edinburgh, 1994).

Stewart, H.B., 'Air Ambulance', *BEA Magazine*, December 1951.

Stroud, John, 'Post War Propliners: Islander and Trislander', *Aeroplane Monthly*, August 1994.

Stroud, John, 'Tamblin's Tram', *Aeroplane Monthly*, March 1997.

Taylor, John, 'Scotland's Air Ambulance Service', *Meccano Magazine*, March 1959. ✈

Acknowledgements

I have received the help of a great number of people and organisations during the compilation of this book.

I am especially grateful to Dr Winifred M. Ewing for writing the Foreword.

Several holidays in Barra had fostered my interest in Barra Airport but it was a letter from John Colledge, the son of Loganair's Jane Colledge, wishing to know something of the airlines which had served the island over the years which actually set me off on the road to recording information about the airport in more detail. Harold and Brenda Couzens, formerly of *Suidheachan*, nurtured this interest and, having lived next to the Tràigh Mhòr for a long time, were able to provide much background material.

Many people at Barra Airport have put up with a lot of questions from me over the years. I would like to record my thanks to Janet MacLean and Jane Colledge of Loganair, and to Keith Rendall and Maggie MacNeil-Campbell of Highlands and Islands Airports Ltd. Keith, before his move to Kirkwall, provided much information about the duties of his staff, of whom Iain 'Lex' MacLean was especially helpful. During a lengthy session at Glasgow Airport, Captain David Dyer, formerly of Loganair and now with British Regional Airlines, gave me the benefit of his experience of many years flying to the Tràigh Mhòr. It is David's photography which adorns the front cover of *Times subject to Tides*.

I am grateful to Fred Barnes for permission to reproduce his article, 'Hebridean Herons', the original version of which appeared in the magazine, *Propliner*, and to Captain Peter Morgan, formerly of BEA, for the description of the occasion when his aircraft became trapped in the sand. David Fowler of Western Isles Libraries, Stornoway, provided many newspaper references from the *Stornoway Gazette* and the *West Highland Free Press*.

The following are due thanks for responding to enquiries and requests for photographs, some upon more than one occasion: Bob Armstrong; Phil Lo Bao; R. A. Beeson; Jamie Bell, Scottish Screen; Dr Bernard Blain; Peter Blinko; Gabrielle Blunt; G. W. Bright; Mrs Anne Cadzow; Catherine Cameron; Peter Collins, Newark Air Museum; Mrs Mona Davidson; Rosemary Dohelsky, Mitchell Library, Glasgow; Bill Dunn; Alasdair D. Falconer; Dr Olive Galbraith; Daniel Green; Captain Vivian Gunton; Cyril Hart; Peter Houghton, formerly of Highlands and Islands Airports Ltd; Dorothy Kidd, Scottish Life Archive, National Museums of Scotland; C. Lever; Mrs M. McDonald; Captain Roddy MacKinnon JP, Councillor for Northbay, Comhairle nan Eilean Siar; Mary Catherine Maclean, Barra Heritage Centre; Neil McNair; Niall MacPherson; Donald Manford; R. Maxwell; R. L. Miles; Captain John L. Morton; Murdo Murray, Comhairle nan Eilean Siar, Stornoway; Tony Naylor; J. F. MacN. Partridge; John Rice; John Stroud; Joe Tweddle; Wilf White; and John Wilson JP.

British Airways Archives and Museum Collection at Heathrow Airport provided references to Barra operations during BEA days, while Scottish Natural Heritage, successor to the Nature Conservancy Council, supplied information about the Eoligarry

Site of Special Scientific Interest reproduced in Appendix 1. The Scottish Office Development Department provided the information about government support for the air service. L. M. Dutton, Manager Aerad, Racal Avionics, gave permission for inclusion of the Barra Airfield runway diagram. Access to the Alasdair Alpin MacGregor photographic collection was courtesy of the Scottish Life Archive of the National Museums of Scotland, Edinburgh. Scott Grier OBE, Chairman of Loganair, provided useful comment on recent Loganair operations to Barra. Douglas Nicolson of Mosfellsbær, Iceland, provided many constructive suggestions for the improvement of the original manuscript. I am grateful to Clive Lewis for pointing me in the right direction when required, and to my sister, Mrs Sybil Cavanagh, and to Richard Battersby, for assisting with proofreading.

Last, but by no means least, I particularly thank Iain Hutchison of Kea Publishing who has brought this book to fruition. He was sure my initial research would be worthy of transformation into the book now before you and he has been a constant source of guidance. Somehow he has always managed to find the time to process continual revisions to text in between studying for exams and family life. Iain has also provided material which appears in the book. ✈

Front cover: Loganair DHC-6 Twin Otter G-BEJP (David Dyer)
Back cover: Tràigh Mhòr from the air, February 1985. (Iain Hutchison)